PRAISE FOR CINDY SHEEHAN

"Cindy Sheehan is a witness in the great tradition of Rosa Parks, Fannie Lou Hamer, and Harriet Tubman."

—REVEREND JESSE JACKSON, quoted in *The Village Voice*

"Cindy Sheehan has become something of a folk hero... Sheehan has a truth to tell, and she has found a way to bring light to what many women know from their gut to be true. With the death of her son, she has been given the gift of clarity that politicians so often lose."

—KELLY MEYER, Cofounder of Women's Cancer Research Fund

"We saw many sparks from the lead-up to the Iraqi war and after the Iraqi war, but when Cindy came to Texas, she was the spark that lit the flame."

—RUSSELL MEANS, Oglala/Lakota, American Indian Movement

"The courage of Cindy Sheehan and all of the families and supporters at Camp Casey are the catalysts that will cause this war to end and will bring our soldiers home. This is a senseless war, and I think America knows that now."

—CONGRESSWOMAN MAXINE WATERS

"Cindy speaks with a combination of utter determination, unassailable integrity, fearlessness, and the peace of someone who knows that their cause is just." —ARIANNA HUFFINGTON

"Cindy is every soldier's mother. If my mom was doing what Cindy Sheehan is doing, I would want someone like me to support her."

—SEAN O'NEILL, Iraq Veterans Against the War

"Perhaps someday a President will greet Cindy Sheehan this way: 'So you're the little woman who stopped the Iraq war.'"

—MIKE GOODWIN, *New York Daily News*

CINDY SHEEHAN

NOT ONE MORE MOTHER'S CHILD

CINDY SHEEHAN

NOT ONE MORE
MOTHER'S CHILD

Koa Books

KIHEI, HAWAI'I AND SANTA FE, NEW MEXICO

Koa Books
P.O. Box 822
Kihei, Maui, Hawai'i 96753

www.koabooks.com

Cover Design by Tom Carling, Carling Design Inc.

Book Design and peace-flag design by Martin Lubin,
Martin Lubin Graphic Design.

Cover Photograph by Jeff Paterson/Not In Our Name.

Special thanks to alternet.org, bradblog.com, buzzflash.com,
commondreams.org, dailykos.com, huffingtonpost.com,
lewrockwell.com, michaelmoore.com, truthout.org, and the other
websites where many of these writings first appeared.

"An Open Letter to George W. Bush" appeared previously in *Stop
the Next War Now*, edited by Medea Benjamin and Jodie Evans
(Inner Ocean Publishing).

ISBN 0-9773338-0-9

Library of Congress Cataloging-in-Publication Data pending

Distributed to the trade by Publishers Group West

CONTENTS

FOREWORD

by Congressman John Conyers, Jr.

A young president once noted the inescapable element of sacrifice in the American endeavor: "Since this country was founded, each generation of Americans has been summoned to give testimony to its national loyalty. The graves of young Americans who answered the call to service surround the globe." Casey Sheehan was only twenty-four years old when he answered his call to service. On April 4, 2004, Casey was on patrol in Baghdad when his unit of the Eighty-second Field Artillery Regiment came under fire. On that day, Casey Sheehan died.

In the face of national tragedy, the public conscience asks a single question: Why? Why are American soldiers embroiled in a war with no cogent plan or realistic exit strategy? Why does the ideology of a very few politicians require the sacrifice of so many soldiers? Why was Cindy Sheehan asked to bury her son?

Shifting storylines and a dissembling spin machine failed to answer this question. And when the time was right, Cindy Sheehan demanded what ought to be the right of any citizen—an audience, however brief, with the public official who owed her an honest response. In the blistering heat of Crawford, Texas, amidst the shouts of protesters and counter-protesters, Cindy Sheehan asked to see the president.

As I write this note from Washington, nearly 2000 American soldiers have died in Iraq. More than 1800 of these men and women have fallen since President Bush, dressed in a military flight suit and walking with the swagger of his convictions, declared our "mission accomplished." The White House has yet to account for an act of such incalculable arrogance. And, as I see it, the president has kept Cindy Sheehan waiting for far too long.

And as she waits, with a mother's patience and a patriot's resolve, her actions are testimony to the truest sort of national loyalty. As the war in Iraq lingers on, American heroes will emerge. Cindy Sheehan is mine.

CINDY: AN HISTORIC PERSPECTIVE

by Thom Hartmann

On October 25, 1998, the British High Court ruled that former Chilean President Augusto Pinochet was not immune from being prosecuted for murder, torture, and genocide. Lord Nicholls wrote the majority opinion of the court, saying: "International law has made it plain that certain types of conduct, including torture and hostage-taking, are not acceptable conduct on the part of anyone. This applies as much to heads of state, or even more so, as it does to anyone else; the contrary conclusion would make a mockery of international law."

Pinochet was being held to account for the illegal war he waged against the "terrorists" he claimed to have found in Chile, because a group of mothers and grandmothers stood up in public—for years—and demanded justice for their missing and dead sons and husbands.

Some of history's most bright and shining moments have been when women have stood up against the insanity of unnecessary war and militaristic persecution.

Abraham Lincoln invited Julia Ward Howe to the White House during the winter of 1861–1862. Soldiers had been singing "John Brown's Body (lies a-mouldering in his grave)" as an informal anthem, and Lincoln was hoping Howe could pen something more appropriate and inspirational for the Union soldiers in that awful war. In one night she wrote what is now known as "The Battle Hymn of the Republic."

For much of the next eight years, Howe worked with organizations caring for the widows, bereft parents, and orphans of the Civil War. She was horrified by war's human, economic, social, and spiritual toll. Using the fame she'd gained from writing the "Battle Hymn," among other things, Howe stood up in 1870 and spoke out for peace, specifically for a national holiday to be called "The Mother's Day for Peace." A faint echo of her proclamation lives on in our Mother's Day.

Howe's proclamation read:

Arise then ... women of this day!
Arise, all women who have hearts!
Whether your baptism be of water or of tears!

Say firmly:
"We will not have questions answered by irrelevant
    agencies,
Our husbands will not come to us, reeking with
    carnage,
For caresses and applause.
Our sons shall not be taken from us to unlearn
All that we have been able to teach them of charity,
    mercy and patience.
We, the women of one country,
Will be too tender of those of another country
To allow our sons to be trained to injure theirs."

From the voice of a devastated Earth a voice goes up
    with
Our own. It says: "Disarm! Disarm!
The sword of murder is not the balance of justice."

Blood does not wipe our dishonor,
Nor violence indicate possession.
As men have often forsaken the plough and the anvil
At the summons of war,
Let women now leave all that may be left of home
For a great and earnest day of counsel.
Let them meet first, as women, to bewail and com-
    memorate the dead.

Let them solemnly take counsel with each other as to
    the means
Whereby the great human family can live in peace...

The Civil War was a terrible and bloody war, and its wounds are still felt today in America. Similarly, the Spanish American War—a war the McKinley Administration lied us into, and after whose administration Karl Rove says he's modeling the Bush presidency—provoked Katherine Lee Bates, who wrote "America the Beautiful," to inspire Mark Twain and other prominent men to protest that war.

With the exception of the Second World War (which was widely seen as a "just war"), every war in American history has produced a strong and vibrant peace movement, and in almost every case women have been at the forefront.

When George W. Bush was using the threat of war with Iraq to shore up Republican chances to regain the Senate in 2002, his bellicose rhetoric provoked the largest outpouring of protest in the history of the world. Ten million people took to the streets to try to make their voices heard. But after the war began, those who opposed Bush's naked lies seemed to lose their way.

Until, that is, Cindy Sheehan stepped forward in the great tradition of the mothers of Chile and Argentina, the women who have protested against war from the times of ancient Greece through every one of America's wars, and of Julia Ward Howe.

Already, of course, Karl Rove has led the charge to "Swift-Boat" Cindy Sheehan. One especially vile email ricocheting across the internet suggests that she had divorced her son's father at an early age and didn't raise her own son. It is, of course, not true. Not even a shred of truth: Cindy gave birth to Casey and she and her husband raised him continuously until he joined the Army in 2000, which was before George W.

Bush had begun ranting about Saddam Hussein, before 9/11, and before the hyper-militarization of the United States. But that doesn't stop the smearing of Cindy Sheehan by the political cons, the war profiteers, and the jingoists. Just as it didn't stop them from attacking Julia Ward Howe and Katherine Lee Bates. On the other hand, being falsely maligned didn't stop Howe, Bates, the women of Argentina and Chile, or Cindy Sheehan.

A dear friend and professor of psychiatry at Harvard Medical School once commented privately to me, "The most dangerous drug in the world is testosterone." To that, I would add, particularly when the man overdosing on it has never actually been in a war zone and thus seen the pain and horrors war brings.

Cindy Sheehan has almost single-handedly reinvigorated the movement in the United States against the Republican War of Choice in Iraq. Throughout the time she has been publicly visible, she has asked a single question: "What is the 'noble cause' for which Casey Sheehan died?"

Although cons, Republicans, and TV talking heads have tried to produce alternative questions and put them in her mouth, this has been her steady focus. And there has not yet been—and most likely never will be—an honest answer to that heartfelt question. The simple truth is that George W. Bush and the Republicans pushed this war to gain "political capital," as Cindy points out in this book.

In *Not One More Mother's Child*, Cindy shares with us her thoughts, motivations, experiences, pains, and joys, and we are all the richer for it. Cindy Sheehan is one of America's heroic figures.

A Personal Introduction

by Jodie Evans

Cindy Sheehan is the mother we all long for. She is nurturing, a she-wolf, a mother bear, unafraid when it comes to the protection of our children. She has empathy; she does not want another mother to experience the pain she is enduring from losing a child needlessly.

Her son Casey went to war to protect those he felt responsible for, the young men who looked to him for guidance and support who, like him, wanted to serve the beautiful values of our country. They did not expect to be betrayed by their government. They did not expect to be sent to a foreign land because of lies.

When I heard Cindy's plan to go to Texas, I was ready to take the next plane to join her. I lost my daughter Lala twenty years ago to a tsunami. Life changes when your child dies. It is an unnatural act. Something makes you fearless—the worst has already happened. Because you can't throw yourself on the grave of your child and be buried with them, you are left to create a life that holds the beauty of your love for them in it.

I arrived in Crawford Sunday, August 7. Cindy had plunked herself down in the ditch the day before. So we all sat in the ditch, being eaten by fire ants and chiggers, enduring ferocious heat, torrential rains, and frightening thunder-and-lightning storms. A broad spectrum of Americans joined us. Some had also experienced the loss of a child, mothers and fathers who had wanted more from their country. Each day, couple after couple, rancher after farmer, vacationing family after student, veterans and their wives came to lend their support.

None of us knew where the vigil would lead. We only knew why we were there, and it was this knowing that held the power. Cindy is a mother looking for answers to very basic questions, questions we all want answered: *You say our children died for a noble cause; what is that noble cause? You keep soldiers there because others have died; WHY? Why do others need to die to justify the deaths of those who have gone before?*

In the first few days of the vigil, many people called with advice, and Cindy was appalled by the manipulations that were suggested—*more flags, more patriotism, don't say this, say that.* Cindy doesn't have a politician's bone in her body. She has her own voice, and she was insulted by those who wanted to change her words and those who thought others were putting words into her mouth. Her responses were lightning-fast, deeply intimate, and full of humor.

Cindy's presence transformed everyone in every moment at Camp Casey. An active-duty solider came to tell her about the importance of her son's mission and his death. Most of us tensed up and tried to keep him from her, but Cindy stepped forward, unafraid of what he might say. She listened, able to hear him and, ultimately, available for his deeper story—that his own mother felt the same as she did. By the end of their conversation, he was calling Cindy "Mom." Her acceptance and capacity to listen changed him, and all of us.

Cindy is common sense. She is Pain personified; she is a mother; she is the voice of common-sense America breaking through the forces of fear. She doesn't have the answers—we elect representatives for that—but she knows the direction that is true. She is someone who will ask a president, generals, and foreign affairs experts to help her find answers.

She doesn't take herself too seriously, although her work is deeply serious, and she expects the same from those who do take themselves too seriously—elected officials, the media, the unaware citizen—who all too often lack any real response to humanity. In our culture, investigation, inquiry, and imagination have been lost to fear, power, and greed. Cindy's is the voice of sanity breaking through the forces of intimidation.

Listen deeply. Cindy speaks with a freshness, an intelligence, and a heart that brings us back to our roots, back to what we love best about ourselves and America. Deeply rooted in America, in her religion, and in her community, Cindy can lead us home, and, in the process, finally bring the soldiers home . . . for good.

I.

WRITINGS
2004-2005

The hardest work of all is trying to digest the fact that the leader of the country your family has fought and died for, for generations, lied to you and betrayed your dear boy's sense of honor and exploited his courage. I'm not politically savvy and I don't have a Karl Rove to plan my strategy, but I do have a big mouth and a righteous cause, which still mean something in this country, I hope.

An Open Letter
to George W. Bush

November 4, 2004

DEAR GEORGE,

You don't mind if I call you George, do you? When you sent me a letter offering your condolences on the death of my son, Spc. Casey Austin Sheehan, in the illegal and unjust war on Iraq, you called me Cindy, so I naturally assume we are on a first-name basis.

George, it has been seven months today since your reckless and wanton foreign policies killed my son, my big boy, my hero, my best friend: Casey. It has been seven months since your ignorant and arrogant lack of planning for the peace murdered my oldest child. It has been two days since your dishonest campaign stole another election, but you all were way more subtle this time than in 2000, weren't you? You hardly had to get the Supreme Court of the United States involved at all this week.

You feel so proud of yourself for betraying the country again, don't you? You think you are very clever, because you pulled the wool over the eyes of some of the people again. You think that you have some mandate from God, you can "spend your political capital" any way that you want. George, you don't care or even realize that 56,000,000-plus citizens of this country voted against you and your agenda. Still, you are going to continue your ruthless work of being a divider and not a uniter. George, in 2000 when you stole that election and the Democrats gave up, I gave up too. I had the most ironic thought of my life then: "Oh well, how much damage can he do in four years?" Well, now I know how much you have damaged my family, this country, and this world. If you think I am going to allow you another four years to do even more damage, then you truly are mistaken. I will fight for a true vote count and, if that fails, your impeachment. Also, the impeachment of your vice president. The only thing is, I'm not politically savvy, and I don't have a Karl Rove to plan my strategy. But I do have a big mouth and a righteous cause, which still mean something in this country, I hope.

All of this lying, fooling, and betraying must be "hard work," George. You really think you know what hard work is?

George, let me tell you what "hard work" really is.

Hard work is seeing your oldest son, your brave and honorable man-child, go off to a war that had, and still has, no basis in reality. Hard work is worrying yourself gray and not being able to sleep for two weeks because you don't know if your child is safe.

Hard work is seeing your son's murder on CNN one Sunday evening while you're enjoying the last supper you'll ever truly enjoy again.

Hard work is having three military officers come to your house a few hours later to confirm the aforementioned murder of your son, your firstborn, your kind and gentle sweet baby.

Hard work is burying your child forty-six days before his twenty-fifth birthday. Hard work is holding your other three children as they lower the body of their big "baba" into the ground. Hard work is not jumping in the grave with him and having the earth cover you both.

But, Dear George, do you know what the hardest work of all is? Trying to digest the fact that the leader of the country that your family has fought for and died for, for generations, lied to you and betrayed your dear boy's sense of honor and exploited his courage and exploited his loyalty to his buddies. Hard work is having your country abandon you after they killed your son. Hard work is coming to the realization that your son had his future robbed from him and that you have had your son's future and future grandchildren stolen from you. Hard work is knowing that there are so many people in this world who have prospered handsomely from your son's death.

George, I must confess that my family and I worked very *hard* to redefeat you this time, but you refuse to stay defeated. Well, we are watching you very carefully. We are going to do everything in our power to have you impeached for misleading the American people into a disastrous war and for misusing and abusing your power as commander-in-chief. We are going to scream until our last breath to bring the rest of our babies home from this quagmire of a war that you have gotten our country into, before too many more families learn the true meaning of hard work. We know it is going to be an uphill battle, knowing how Republican Congress is, but thanks to you, we know the meaning of hard work and we're not afraid of hard work at all.

The 56,000,000-plus citizens who voted against you and your agenda have given me a mandate to move forward with my agenda. Also, thanks to you and your careless domestic policies, I am unemployed, so this will be my full-time job. Bringing about your political downfall will be the noblest accomplishment of my life, and it will bring justice for my son and 1125 (so far) other brave Americans and tens of thousands of innocent Iraqis your lies have killed. By the way, George, how many more innocent Iraqis are your policies going to kill before you convince them that you are better than Saddam?

How many more of their cities are you going to level before you consider that they are liberated? If you really had any moral values or if you were an honorable man at all, you would resign. My son was a man who had high moral values and true courage. Humanity lost a bright light on April 4, 2004. I will live the rest of my life missing Casey desperately. Thank you for that, George. Have a nice day.

God Bless America!! We surely need it!

Cindy Sheehan

Casey's Story

My son Casey Austin Sheehan was born on May 29, 1979. After a long labor, he was born on Memorial Day. I would look into his eyes and see a depth of wisdom there from the time he was born. He was born with an "old soul." As a proud mom, I knew, and I would tell everyone who would listen to me, that he was going to be a great man. I was right. I just didn't realize how great he was going to be, or how much his moment of greatness was going to hurt me.

Casey was a very good baby. From the time he was about seven months old and had gone into his own room, he would wake up in the morning and talk to himself and play with his crib gym. His dad and I would lie in our room and listen to him play. When he learned to walk, he would come up behind me when I would be doing the dishes and he would throw his arms around my legs, kiss me on the butt, and say, "I wuv you mama." He had a little teddy bear that he called "Bear." He ate all the fur off of it and he ate all the fuzz from the inside of it. He wouldn't go to bed without it, though. I still have his bear and it is now sitting on the shelf by the flag that was draped over his coffin.

Casey was our firstborn. We had three more children after him: Carly, Andy, and Janey. Their dad, my husband Pat, made our family of six complete. We did everything together. The kids went to Catholic school together. Even when one of us would want a frozen yogurt, we would all pile into "Vanna White," our white Chevy Astro Van, and we would go to Bellflower, to Yogurt Lee, together. There was no such thing as one of us going and bringing yogurt home for everybody. We all just went.

On most Friday nights, we would have "Chicks and Dudes" night. After a long week of work, school, and other activities, we would go out to dinner, usually at Chris and Pitts in Bellflower, where you could get a good and filling barbeque dinner for about $25 for our entire family of six. Anyway, we would go home and watch TGIF on ABC. *Full House* and the show that Steve Urkel was on were among the shows on TGIF. The "Chicks," Carly, Janey, and I, would go in the parents' room to watch TGIF; the "Dudes," Pat, Casey, and Andy, would stay in the living room and watch the shows. The kids still remember those nights fondly, the boys having some quality time with their dad and the girls doing the same with their mom.

Casey was always a good boy. He could play for hours by himself. He loved Nintendo, G.I. Joes, World Wrestling Federation, baseball (especially the Dodgers), his church, and God. He joined Cub Scouts when he was in first grade and he eventually earned the rank of Eagle Scout. He became an altar boy when he was eight and he continued serving his church for the rest of his life. He loved to act and was in the International Thespian Society when he was in high school. Before he joined the Army, he earned an A.A. degree in drama. He was a reporter for his college newspaper. He never talked back to his dad or me. He rarely fought with his brother and sisters. He loved our animals and he loved little children.

Everyone assumed Casey was going to be a priest, because he was so faithful to God and to the church. He never missed mass, even when he went into the Army. If he was on post, he went to mass. He served his church in every capacity that a layperson can. He also was very involved with the youth ministry of our parish, especially when I was the youth minister. Even after he graduated from high school, he stayed active in the ministry, helping me as a young-adult leader. Casey confided in me, though, that he wanted to get married and have children. He hoped one day to be a permanent deacon in the church. Deacons can get married and serve the church in various ways. Casey also confided to me that he was a virgin and he wanted to save himself and give his virginity to his wife as a wedding present. He took lots of heat for that in the Army. Pat and I always wondered why he would even tell anyone he was still a virgin, but he did. His buddies would say, "Sheehan, you gotta get laid." He would just say, "Naw, that's okay."

Casey was such a good Christian and good Catholic that when his chapel at Fort Hood started a new Knights of Columbus Council, they named it the Spc. Casey Austin Sheehan Council. The brother Knights told Pat and me that he embodied everything that they want to stand for: Love of God, Country, Family, Church, and Service. Pat and I were honored that they would name their council after Casey. Casey's name and what he stood for will always be remembered at Fort Hood. The Knights were going to name their new council after a priest who had served there for quite awhile, but after they heard about Casey's heroic sacrifice, they decided to name the council after him. They voted unanimously to do this.

Casey joined the Army in May 2000. His recruiter told him that he would be able to finish college, be a chaplain's assistant, receive a $20,000 signing bonus, and most insidiously and heartbreakingly, never see combat. Casey scored so high on the ASVAB (military competency test) that he would be only in a support role, and he would never be in a battle. Well, Casey's recruiter broke every single promise he made. The only one

I care about, though, is the one where Casey would never see battle.

Casey's division, the First Cavalry Division out of Fort Hood, was sent to Iraq in March 2004. He called home once from Kuwait on March 14. He said he was hot, they had been busy getting ready to convoy to Baghdad, and he was on his way to mass (naturally). His company, Charlie Battery, convoyed peacefully to Baghdad and reached its post, F.O.B. War Eagle in Sadr City, on March 19. On April 4, Palm Sunday, we got the word that Casey had been killed in an ambush. The first chance he got, my brave, wonderful, faithful, sweet, gentle, and kind boy volunteered for a rescue mission as a Combat Life Saver. He was a Humvee mechanic who never should have gone on a mission like that. Casey and twenty of his buddies were sent into a raging insurgent uprising to rescue wounded soldiers. Only thirteen of them returned. Casey was riding in the back of a trailer with no protection when they were ambushed. He was killed within minutes of the ambush. He was able to return fire and buy some time for his unit. His actions that day saved lives. Casey is a hero who belongs to history now, but I wish he were a living, breathing coward so I could still talk to him, e-mail him, send him care packages and Christmas presents, hug him, and never let go when he got back from the war.

This war has devastated my family, but especially me. My sweet boy who never passed up a chance to kiss my behind and tell me he "wuvs" me is gone forever. God, I hope this war ends before other mothers have to go through this. I hope this world survives four more years of the lies and betrayals of this president. Eventually, this war will end, as all wars end. This president will either bumble through four more years, or he will do something so egregious that he will be impeached. But when this nightmare is over for the world, it will go on for me. Forever, and ever, without end. Amen.

The Dangerous Gold Star Families

I am one of the founding members of a group called Gold Star Families for Peace. We who have lost loved ones in this illegal and immoral war in Iraq have organized to use our collective voices to bring the tragedy of war to the forefront of America's hearts and souls, as it so tragically is in ours. We are amazed that so few of our fellow citizens are touched by the horrors of the invasion and occupation of a sovereign country. It seems to us like the only people who are asked to sacrifice anything for the war effort are our brave young men and women fighting this so-called war, and their families. There are some families in our nation who, like us, have paid the ultimate price for the lies and betrayals of this current administration.

I, and some other Gold Star Families, have been writing and calling the Department of Defense. We were meeting in D.C. to protest the inauguration, and we thought it would be a good time to meet with Donald Rumsfeld. We have many questions to ask him about our loved ones' deaths, and we deserve to have some answers. I think it is our right as Americans and grieving families to have these answers. For example, why were the children of this country sent to fight a war without the proper training, equipment, or armor? Why were our children sent to fight a war that had no basis in reality? Why are American children still over there fighting a war, and dying in a war, when all the reasons for the war have been proven false? When is this administration going to bring the rest of our children home before it's too late for their families?

If we had been granted an audience with him, we didn't really expect Mr. Rumsfeld to be truthful with us, or even polite, considering his past history of being so sarcastically untruthful and blatantly rude. The real reason I wanted to meet with Rumsfeld was so he could see the face of my son,

Spc. Casey Sheehan, who was killed in Sadr City on 04/04/04. I wanted him to look me in the face and see my red swollen eyes and to see all the lines that grief has etched. I wanted him to see the unbearable pain his ignorance and arrogance have caused my family and me. I wanted him to know that his actions have terrible consequences.

Our letters, phone calls, faxes, and e-mails to the Pentagon were to no avail: we received no response. So, in conjunction with Military Families Speak Out, we decided to go to the Pentagon and try to meet with someone, anyone. We were met at the parking lot by a couple of dozen police officers blocking our way. We were told that we weren't allowed to go into the Pentagon because we didn't go through the proper protocol to request a meeting!!

I find it ironic that with all the tight security for the events in D.C. that week, the time and energy were mustered to forcefully stop families in mourning from entering the Pentagon. I also find it ironic that if I were a wealthy Republican who had donated large sums of money for the "re"-election of the president, I could have had access to all the bigwigs at the lavish parties, but I, whose son paid the ultimate price of his precious life to this country, can't even get within a half of a mile of the man who sent him to die.

We Gold Star Families for Peace are not giving up the fight to hold someone in this administration accountable for the quagmire in Iraq and the more important struggle to bring the rest of our children home from this devastating occupation now. It takes most of our energy just to get out of our beds in the morning and mourn our horrific losses. We need all Americans to wake up and start lobbying their elected officials for an end to this immorality in Iraq and to join our voices in protest.

MY "VACATION" IN FLORIDA

I flew into Florida the week before the 2004 presidential election, not knowing what I would find there. What I found was a rich dichotomy of ideas and political theologies. I was called names, and I was praised as a brave patriot. Some people who looked at my picture of Casey wept for my pain and for the tragedy of his death. And others smirked for the shame of my campaigning against a president they regard as strong on terror and pro-life. The people who smirked wouldn't look at Casey's picture. They didn't want to put a face on this senseless war that they support.

Republicans in Florida invariably reminded me that my son "volunteered" to go to war. They never (with the exception of ten-year-old Tanner in Pensacola) expressed any kind of sympathy or compassion. Yes, Casey did enlist and re-enlist in the Army. He loved being a soldier, and he loved his buddies. He was a good soldier, and he volunteered for the dangerous mission he was killed on. He was a trusting person, and he trusted his commander-in-chief to use his troops with great care, to send them into harm's way only if there is a clear-and-present danger to our country. But this commander-in-chief has misused and abused his position of authority and put our troops in a preemptive war that has no basis in reality. Bush exploited Casey's sense of duty and honor and sent him to a war for domination of the Middle East and profiteering by his cronies. While I was in Florida, I heard Dick Cheney give a speech, and he said, "Iraq has been a remarkable success story." Sure—for Halliburton, Exxon, Osama Bin Laden, Moqtada al-Sadr, Ayad Allawi, Saudi Arabia, and Iran.

At the Cheney rally, a most discouraging thing happened. I was standing by a symbolic coffin with two other families who also lost loved ones. We were holding pictures of our brave children, and a Republican walked by, looked at our signs, and said, "Hmmm, I came back." What could he possibly have meant? Does "I came back" mean, "Ha-ha, your son didn't"? or, "I must've been a better soldier than your son"? Whatever he meant, it hurt us deeply. And he wasn't the only one among the Bush/Cheney supporters who treated us in such an uncaring way.

But I also met progressives who were filled with energy and commitment to defeating Bush—motivated, caring, and compassionate; sorry for my son's sacrifice and for what our family is going through; and grateful that I came all the way from California to help. They were young and old people who have had enough of the lies and abuse of power and want their democracy back.

I went to Florida to make a difference. I went up and down the state doing interviews and joining protests and peace marches. I left my home and my family to try and make the world a better place, just as Casey did. If I didn't do everything I could to deprive the man who has devastated our world and my family of another term in office, I wouldn't have been able to look myself or my other three children in the face.

On April 4, 2004, I lost all hope. Devastated by the murder of my oldest child, I went into a valley of despair. I would like the amazing progressive movement in Florida to know that I am eternally grateful to them for helping me climb out of this valley and restoring my hope.

We will take our country back and get our troops home!

NOT WORTH MY SON'S SACRIFICE

In January 2005, I was asked to be on the *Larry King Live* show to offer my opinion on the election in Iraq from the perspective of a mom whose son was killed in the war prior to the elections. One of the questions I was going to be asked was: Do I think my son's sacrifice was "worth it"? I didn't get a chance to be on the show, though, because I was bumped for something *really* important: the Michael Jackson trial.

If I had been allowed to go on *Larry King Live* and give my opinion about the elections and about my son's sacrifice, this is what I would have told Mr. King and his viewers:

My son, Spc. Casey Austin Sheehan (KIA, Sadr City, 04/04/04), enlisted in the Army to protect America and give something back to our country. He didn't enlist to be used and misused by a reckless commander-in-chief who sent his troops to preemptively attack and occupy a country that was no imminent threat (or any threat) to our country. Casey was sent to die in a war that was based on the imagination of some neocons who love to fill our lives with fear.

Casey didn't agree with the "Mission," but being the courageous and honorable man that he was, he knew he had to go to this mistake of a war to support his buddies. Casey also wondered aloud many times why precious troops and resources were being diverted from the real war on terror.

Casey was told that he would be welcomed to Iraq as a liberator with chocolates and rose petals strewn in front of his unarmored Humvee. He was in Iraq for two short weeks when the Shiite rebel "welcome wagon" welcomed him to Baghdad with bullets and rocket-propelled grenades that took his young and beautiful life. I think my son's helmet and Vietnam-era flak jacket would have protected him better from the chocolates and flower petals.

Casey was killed after George Bush proclaimed "Mission Accomplished" on May 1, 2003, and he was killed after Saddam was captured in December of that same year. Casey was killed before the transfer of power in June 2004 and before these elections. Four marines were tragically killed after the election. By my count, about five dozen Iraqis and coalition troops were killed on election day—is that the definition of "catastrophic success"? But is that a good day in Iraq? Hundreds of our young people and thousands of Iraqis have been needlessly and senselessly murdered since George Bush triumphantly announced an end to "major combat" almost two years ago now. All of the above events have been heralded by this administration as "turning points" in the "war on terror"—or as wonderful events in the "march of democracy." Really? I don't think, judging by very recent history, that the elections will stop the bloodshed and destruction.

I would have asked Mr. King if he would want to sacrifice one of his children for sham elections in Iraq. Would he or George Bush send their children to be killed, or maimed for life, for a series of lies, mistakes, and miscalculations? Now that every lie for the invasion and occupation of Iraq has been exposed to the light: why are our sons and daughters still there? *Not one more drop of blood should be spilled for this pack of lies!*

This war was sold to the American people by a slimy leadership with a maniacal zeal and phony sincerity that would have impressed snake-oil salesmen a century ago. The average American needs to hear from people who have been devastated by the arrogance and ignorance of an administration that doesn't even have the decency or compassion to sign our death letters.

In the interest of being "fair and balanced" (oops, wrong network), *Larry King Live* would have pitted me against a parent who still agrees with the "Mission" and the president. Although, I grieve for that parent's loss and I respect that parent's opinion, I would have defied Mr. King or that parent to explain the "Mission" to me. I don't think anyone can do it with a straight face. The president has also stated that we need to keep our troops in Iraq to honor our sacrifices by completing this elusive and ever changing "Mission." My response to him is, "Just because it is too late for Casey and the Sheehan family, why would we want another innocent life taken in the name of this chameleon of a 'Mission'?"

Well, I was bumped from the show anyway. Now that Scott Peterson has been convicted and sentenced for his crimes and Laci and Connor's families have the justice they deserve, we have the new "trial of the century" to keep our minds off of the nasty and annoying fact that we are waging an immoral war in Iraq. We can fill our TV screens and homes with the glorified images of the Michael Jackson molestation trial. We can fill our lives with outrage over MJ's victims and hope they get justice, not even questioning the fact that George Bush, his dishonest cabinet, and their misguided policies aren't even brought to the court of public opinion. We won't have to confront ourselves with the fact that the leaders of our country and their lies are responsible for the deaths of 1438 brave Americans—and tens of thousands of innocent Iraqis—and the loss of our nation's credibility throughout the world. That might mean we would have to turn off our television sets and do something about it.

In answer to the original question, Larry: No, it wasn't worth it!!

THE AMAZING HYPOCRITES

March 2005 marked the two-year anniversary of the beginning of "Shock and Awe" of the U.S. government's aggression in Iraq. If you only watched CNN, FOX News, or MSNBC, you wouldn't have known that there were protests all across our nation. CNN called the over eight hundred protest events "barely a ripple." I spoke at a protest in Fayetteville, North Carolina, where there were right around four thousand people full of energy and committed to the task of peace and justice and reclaiming our country from the sociopathic maniacs in power.

So what were the hypocrites in D.C. doing while much of the country was working for peace—at rallies, marches, and candlelight vigils? They were conducting an emergency smoke-screen session in Congress to draft legislation for one woman: Terry Schiavo. Terry's story is tragic, and her family suffered unbearable pain for many years with her "persistent vegetative" state. I feel so much compassion for her mother, who had to watch her daughter slowly waste away. My heart truly breaks for everyone in Terry Schiavo's family.

But I do have one question for Congress and for George ("When in doubt, it is always better to err on the side of life"— March 22, 2005) Bush, though: Why does Terry Schiavo deserve to live more than my son, Spc. Casey Austin Sheehan, did? Casey was misused and abused by his commander-in-chief and executive branch that boldly lied to the American public and the less gullible citizens of other countries about the reasons for the invasion of Iraq.

Casey was sent to Iraq to be killed by the same pack of cowards and murderers who so "valiantly" and tirelessly fought for the right for Ms. Schiavo to live! The green light for Casey's murder was given by a Congress who expediently abrogated their constitutional rights to a president whose foreign policies are not based on reality or even loosely based on any kind of Christian moral values. Someone needs to give Congress basic lessons on the Constitution: declaring war—*yes*; meddling in a family's private tragedy—*no!!*

As far as I am concerned, the amazing hypocrites in our government are not making up for killing thousands of innocent Americans and Iraqis by passing emergency legislation to save one life. Every member of Bush's executive branch (past and present) and every member of Congress who voted to give George the authority to invade Iraq have innocent blood on their hands. For the next State of the Union address, maybe the hypocrites in Congress should shamefacedly display blood-soaked hands instead of proudly wriggling fingers stained with ink to symbolize sham Iraqi elections.

Instead of a culture of life, this administration has promoted the opposite: from Bush's signing into Texas law the Futile Care Bill, to the culture of the death penalty in Texas (and around our nation), proposed cuts in Medicaid, and laws restricting medical malpractice lawsuits and Chapter 7 bankruptcy for families who have incurred huge medical bills. Members of this shameful Congress should go back on vacation and go back to their home districts and look for people who have been devastated by the illegal occupation of Iraq.

Mr. Tom ("We should investigate every avenue before we take the life of a living human being") DeLay should be outraged for the soldiers who have been murdered for the cowardice of him and his colleagues. He should shed real tears for the soldiers' families whose lives have been destroyed by their murders. DeLay should search for a homeless Iraq vet and pass legislation to find him a job and an apartment. Mr. Tom (who cried over Ms. Schiavo's hunger pains) DeLay should go to Walter Reed Hospital and find one of our kids who has been horribly maimed by the betrayal of his government and pass legislation to pay for his meals—after three months, the wounded soldier has to pay for his meals with his own money. Maybe Mr. Tom (Crocodile Tears) DeLay should find a soldier who has returned from this abomination of a war who is suffering from PTSD and pass a law to get him the help he needs before the soldier's dad finds him hanging by a garden hose in the basement.

Maybe if Tom DeLay and the rest of the members of Congress who voted for the Terry Schiavo Emergency Relief Act and who voted to give George Bush the authority to go to war and who voted to give George Bush more money to waste in Iraq sought out and talked to us citizens whose lives have been tragically impaired by the invasion/occupation of Iraq and could hear our stories, they might rush back to D.C. to vote to rip the authority out of the president's hands and end the immoral occupation of Iraq. One thing this "Circus of Hypocrisy" has shown me is that Congress can accomplish something when it sets its mind to it. Now it is time to accomplish something important—and I am not talking about steroids use in baseball.

I have a great idea!! Although Mr. Tom (Politician Protection Act: HB 913) DeLay is not my congressman (hmmm—don't think he's Terry Schiavo's congressman, either), maybe I should ask him to introduce the Soldiers Put in Harm's Way for Lies and Betrayals Emergency Relief Act—and force the amazing hypocrites to bring our troops home, now!!

NAME WITHHELD
PENDING NOTIFICATION

When I woke up this morning (May 8, 2005), the "official" death count in Iraq was 1576. The first thing I do in the morning after I turn on my computer is to check the Department of Defense website to see if any more of our nation's precious children were killed in this horror of a nonsensical war. I was talking to another Gold Star mom, Celeste Zappala, today, and she sadly advised me that the count rose to 1579 while she was out to lunch.

Celeste and I and too many other moms know what the significance of "Pending Notification" means. It means that there are people in our country going through their lives right now not even knowing that they are about to be ambushed with the most devastating news of their lives: "We regret to inform you..."

Somewhere in America, there is a mom (I always think of the moms first) shopping for groceries, driving home from a long week of work, or maybe even planning her soldier's homecoming party. Somewhere, here in our country, there is a mother who is hoping that she will receive a Mother's Day card from her soldier, or perhaps, if she is extremely lucky, a rushed telephone call. There is a mom out there who has been worried sick about her soldier since they arrived in the combat zone. Maybe the mom still supports George Bush and the occupation, or maybe the mom is certain that if her child is killed in this abomination, her sweet baby, her soldier, will have died for lies and betrayals. In the end, and at that moment, the mom is not going to care about politics or about reasons for invasion and occupation. She won't care if her child died for freedom and democracy, or to make some people wealthier and more powerful. All she will see is the Grim Reaper in a uniform standing at her door before she collapses on the floor screaming for her child and pleading with the Grim Reaper to take her with him.

Somewhere there is a father in America who won't know what hit him and who won't know whom to hit back. There are brothers and sisters, nieces and nephews, spouses, and children who are about to step on the path of unbearable pain and seemingly endless grief. Today there are the families and friends of three wonderful human beings who never, until now, knew that the human body could produce so many tears. Somewhere in America live our fellow citizens who never even knew that a broken heart is not theoretical or symbolic. These most unfortunates are about to find out that a broken heart hurts far worse than a broken limb, and does not heal so readily, if ever at all.

The families of these soldiers are also departing on a long tour of banalities uttered by well-meaning, but let's face it, uninformed people. I hear these phrases over and over again: "Time heals everything," "Casey's in a better place" (oh, really, I didn't know that home with his mom was such a bad place to be), "Casey wants you to be happy," "Casey died doing what he loved doing" (he did?), or my favorite, "Casey died defending his country." Let me assure the reader, phrases like this do not help. They are clichés, for one thing, and for another, none of them are true. None of them help a grieving family. If you, the reader, are ever in the situation facing a mom who had her son brutally murdered, God forbid, I will give you hints on what does help: hugs (lots and lots), make sure she eats, make sure she drinks plenty of water (tears are dehydrating), make sure she hears wonderful things about her child, bring boxes of tissues and toilet paper, and bring yourself. Leave your tired and impotent clichés at the door.

Of course, the most tragic thing about the 1579 is that not even one should be dead. Our "president" cheerfully rushed this country into a needlessly horrendous and devastating invasion. Our "president" thinks stolen elections confer a mandate.

Our Congress cheerfully relinquished their constitutional responsibility to declare war. If they had any courage or honor, they would claim that right back and end this travesty. I have a feeling our mis-leaders will be having a nice day with their moms or their children on Mother's Day. As they are eating their brunches and giving and receiving bouquets of Mother's Day flowers, they probably never even think about the moms in this world that their insanely reckless policies have destroyed. It never enters their wicked brains that they have ruined Mother's Day for so many families. This is a tragedy.

Our media was, and still is, a willing shill for the administration and has never told the American public the truth. Reporting about Iraq is always trumped by child molesters, Martha Stewart, Terri Schiavo, Scott Peterson, the American Idol, and Runaway Brides. Another tragic thing about this illegal and disastrous invasion and occupation is that there are only 1579 families in this country who even have to think about Iraq. Most Americans probably don't even know where to find Iraq on a map. The Halliburtons, Bechtels, KBRs, and oil oligarchs of the world, who are laughing all the way to the bank, think of Iraq with greedy glee each day. Sorrowfully, there are 1579 families in this country who have "Iraq" carved on their hearts and souls for eternity. We have sacrificed more than the $1.99 it costs to buy a "Support the Troops" magnet for our cars. We have had a violent amputation. Even if our fellow citizens don't realize it, by allowing this occupation to continue, they are also losing a very important part of themselves: their humanity.

My heart, my prayers, and my love go to the three families who are now embarking on this mournful, unnecessary journey. We at Gold Star Families for Peace are here for them. I hope they find comfort in what I know now seems like a comfortless world. Peace.

STILL NOT WORTH IT
LARRY KING, PART 2

In January, I was bumped from the *Larry King Live* show in favor of an appearance by the soon-to-be-proved-innocent alleged pedophile, Michael Jackson. I was going to be on the program to answer the question: Did I feel my son's murder in Iraq was "worth it" after the January 30 "free" elections in that war-torn country? That's when I wrote the article, "Not Worth my son's sacrifice."

I never thought I would be invited back on as a guest after I pretty much burned the Larry King bridge with my article. However, to my astonishment, I was invited back to be a guest on June 28. I was asked to be on the broadcast to give my impressions and rebuttal to George's speech on Iraq that he delivered in front of the less-than-enthusiastic (what the White House spin doctors call "respectful") troops at Fort Bragg, North Carolina.

I felt like I was in Bizarro World as I heard George speak about 9/11 five times and mention terrorism thirty-one times, even though these rationales for war have been disproved repeatedly. I think George thinks that since we believed him once about terrorism vis-à-vis Iraq, we must be gullible enough to believe him this time. I don't know, and I am not a professional pundit, but my theory is that he might have mentioned 9/11 to manipulate our emotions and maybe even frighten us a little again.

The thing that struck me when I was watching that vacuous man giving his hollow speech was the fact that he could have always replaced the word "terrorists" with the phrase "my moronic and callous foreign policies." For example, when he said that terrorists spread death and destruction on the streets of Baghdad and kill innocent people, he could have just as easily said, "My moronic and callous foreign policies spread death and destruction on the streets of Baghdad and kill innocent people." When he said that we need to stop terrorists from toppling governments in the region, he could just as easily have said, "We need to stop my moronic and callous foreign policies from toppling governments in the region." People have characterized the speech-lite in many ways, but if I had to pick a few words to describe it, I would say, "Hypocritical, manipulative, condescending, meaningless drivel."

I sat through an entire hour in the CNN studio in D.C. not hearing one person say that the invasion was a mistake and if it was a mistake, then our troops should be brought home immediately. Even the "Democratic" senators (Kerry and Bayh) who were on the program just gave their recipes for "success" in Iraq, which did not include any exit strategies. The guest host for that hour was Bob Costas, and he asked one guest, Senator John McCain, an intriguing question, "If you could push Button One and have an eventual wonderful outcome in Iraq, or if you could push Button Two and never have had it happen, which one would you pick?" Of course, Senator McCain chose Button One. He hasn't had a loved one killed in this enormous tragedy of a war, nor does he have a loved one in harm's way. It has not affected him personally one bit. What skin is it off McCain's teeth if our troops remain for a highly unlikely rosy outcome at the cost of thousands of more lives? I would push the button that would bring back my son, Casey, and the tens of thousands of the others who have been killed for nothing but outright lies and bald-faced betrayals. I would push the button that would give Iraq back its power, water, and infrastructure.

My absolute favorite guest of the evening was Senator John Warner, powerful chair of the Senate Armed Disservices Committee. Of course, he fell in lockstep behind his fuehrer and praised the speech and how, although we have "all" paid a terrible price for this invasion and occupation, bringing freedom and democracy to the Iraqi people is worth all the sacrifices that the world is making. I sat in the Green Room with Senator Warner's entourage. I wondered (even out loud) what price they have paid for our administration's misdeeds in Iraq. They all looked like happy, well-fed, well-dressed, well-educated, and well-hydrated Americans. They looked to me like they had plenty of electricity to blow-dry their hair and charge their cell phones and laptops. They looked like they had quite a nice supply of clean drinking water and fresh food. I sincerely doubt if any of them had a loved one ripped from their lives by a car bomb, an improvised explosive device, or a bullet in an ambush. I wondered who the "we" was that John Warner spoke of. I spoke with John Warner after his interview and told him that unless he was prepared to sacrifice even a good night's sleep over this senseless and criminal war, then he should work on ending it, not prolonging the carnage. He told me that I was "entitled to my opinion," but he would respectfully have to disagree with me. That was awfully constitutional of him!

I finally got on to speak for my eighty-two seconds (all the time *Larry King Live* could spare for the peace message) about how this war is a catastrophe and how we should bring the troops home and quit forcing the Iraqi people to pay for our government's hubris and quit forcing innocent children to suffer so we can fight terrorism somewhere besides America. How absolutely racist and immoral is it to take America's battles to another land and make an entire country pay for the crimes of others? To me, this is blatant genocide. How dare we export our patriotic brand of flag-waving death and devastation to a people who have been through so much already? It wasn't bad enough that our sanctions killed tens of thousands of Iraqis before we even started an active aggression among them—now we have to create confusion, chaos, and disorder there. How dare our president, Congress, and we Americans allow this to continue?

After my brief advocacy for peace, my position was refuted by another mom whose son was killed in Iraq in 2003, who said she "totally disagrees" with me and "feels sorry" for me. Well, you know what? I ache for her blindness and for the millions of sheeple who have had the wool pulled over their eyes by the bunch of hypocritical, bad shepherds who are running disastrous herd over the world. I have distressing news for the Soccer Safety Moms and the NASCAR Dads who are such ardent supporters of this administration and war: Your grandchildren and children who will be entering kindergarten this fall will be fighting George's endless war if he gets his way and is allowed to continue spreading the cancer of imperialism in the Middle East. Donny Rumsfeld said we could be in Iraq for another dozen years. Does anybody think that with all the billions of dollars being poured into constructing super-sized bases in Iraq that the war machine plans on relinquishing the cash cow that is that poor, unfortunate land anytime soon? Think about it when you tuck your child into bed tonight.

I heard George and the senators say that evening that the sacrifices we as Americans have had to make for Iraq are "worth it." I really would like to know who has benefited and profited from Iraq and who has really had to sacrifice anything. I know it was "worth it" to Dick Cheney, who was the CEO of Halliburton (of no-bid contract fame), which has raped billions of dollars from our government, from the people of Iraq, and from our soldiers who are not getting what they need to survive in a combat zone. It is "worth it" to Black Water Security Company, which sends $1000-a-day mercenaries to Iraq, funded by the War Department. It is "worth it" to L. Paul Bremer, under whose watch $8.8 *billion* went missing from the Provisional Authority. It is also "worth it" to the other companies and individuals who have been enriched by feeding our children to the military-industrial complex. By George, I think we have found the people who think this war is "worth it." But is it worth it to George Bush, who was counting on this unlawful and unprincipled aggression in Iraq to give him "political capital"? Instead, if poll numbers are any good indication, Americans are withdrawing their assent for George, and they are withdrawing their consent for him to wage eternal war on humanity.

As I sat in the Green Room of CNN, I was saddened and troubled by George's call for us Americans to fly the flag proudly on July 4 to honor our troops. For one thing, the American flag is not a magical token that can bring armor to the troops who are still dying without the protection. The flag is not a faith healer that can restore limbs and eyesight to the ones who have been maimed forever. The flag is not a genie in a bottle who can blink her eyes and bring our children home from this horrible blunder that they are suffering for and being slaughtered for. But as for me, I will never be able to celebrate another patriotic holiday without mourning what this nation has stolen from my family. I will never be able to look at an American flag without thinking of the uniform my son wore proudly that displayed that same symbol, and the evil ones who desecrated and defiled the stars and stripes by lying us into the invasion of Iraq. No, Casey's sacrifice was not "worth it," and George needs to do more than wave his flag and manipulate our sense of patriotism. He needs to march his girls to a recruitment center and send them to Iraq to fight the terrorists that his moronic and callous foreign policies have recruited, or he needs to wake up and smell the apple pie and bring our other sons and daughters home now!

UNCONSCIONABLE RECRUITING

Lisa from Washington State writes:

"My son-in-law in Iraq said they are being pressured round the clock to re-enlist or face stop loss. They are being offered $30,000 signing bonus, tax-free, and told if they don't re-enlist, they are going to be stop-lossed and get zero dollars. They are pushing the troops round the clock and Mark only got three hours sleep in forty-eight hours and when they get back, they are faced yet again with re-enlisting. Mark said many guys are scared and signing up, and their families at home are very upset (with good reason). We really need to push our media and congressmen to expose the horrible way our troops are being treated."

Lietta, also from Washington State, writes:

"Yes, I have been trying since January '05 to get the word out regarding my own two loved ones and the soldiers in their division. Both served in Iraq, and their division, First Armored, was the first to be 'extended,' so they served fifteen months in Iraq, April '03–July '04. They came back to their bases in August '04. A mere five months later, January '05, their division was told they were under orders to redeploy to Iraq and stop-lossed and would redeploy in Fall '05. And I have been trying to call attention to the 'retention' practices ever since.

"March '05, it was time for both to make decision to re-enlist. As already under orders to redeploy—as already under stop loss—their choices = (1) don't re-enlist but you will wind up in Iraq anyway under stop loss, or (2) re-enlist and while you'll still wind up in Iraq under stop loss, at least you'll have the attractive bonus being offered.

"The point is that the 'retention rate' that is being touted as demonstrative of soldiers' fervor and good faith in the war is another deception being foisted on the media and public. Closer to the truth of the situation is that once they are in, they cannot get out, and it is entrapment from the front end with deceptive recruitment practices, again at re-enlistment time with the threat of deployment to Iraq under stop loss, again when contract ends and they are kept in and deployed via stop loss. What continues to be called an 'all-voluntary military' has become an 'involuntary' military through the use strategies of deception and legal maneuvering for which there seems to be no remedy in the stop loss."

Tia from Baltimore writes (her stepson was KIA in Iraq):

"But I will never forget one thing: the day we dropped David off for boot camp—the day his father and I first met the recruiter—the recruiter put out his hand, smiled at me, shook my hand and said, 'You'll never have to worry about him again.' I was shocked. I can only speculate what this person was telling David."

These are not isolated stories from the illegal occupation, but they are illustrative of what is happening to our young people who thought they were doing the right and honorable thing by enlisting in the military. This is an immoral war that our troops never should have been sent to in the first place, and once they are there and have done their time, it is very difficult for them to get out of the distant mental desert and come home to their loved ones.

Not only are the back-end policies of retention shady, but the front-end policies of recruiting our vulnerable youth are often downright unethical. Few citizens in our country realize (I know I didn't) that an enlistment contract *is binding only on the recruit.* Once the recruit raises his or her right hand and swears allegiance to the government, that recruit becomes the property of Uncle Sam and is bound by the Uniform Code of Military Justice. Ethics, promises, and moral correctness often fly out the window as servitude, hardship, and heartache fly in.

The only recruiting story I know by heart and can effectively comment on is my son Casey's. I have heard too many similar stories, however. When he was recruited in May 2000, he was promised the moon to get him to join, and he ultimately got an early grave. He was promised a $20,000 signing bonus: he received $4500 and was told that he could use the rest for college. Casey wanted to be a deacon in the Catholic Church, so when he enlisted in the Army, he was promised he could be a chaplain's assistant (don't believe the Army band stories, either). When he got to boot camp, he was told that his promised specialty wasn't open, and he had the choice of being a Humvee mechanic or a cook. His recruiter told him he could finish college while in the military; he could never get approval to take even one class.

All of these broken promises mean nothing to me. One does, however. After Casey enlisted, he knew I was upset. He told me, "Mom, you don't have to worry, Sergeant (I forget his name) told me that since I scored so high on the ASVAB (military competency) test, I will never see combat, even if there is a war. I will only be in a support role."

I can still hear his voice saying those exact words to me. Those words chilled me to the bone then, and have haunted me since 9/11. First of all, because I thought Casey would be sent to fight terrorists wherever they might be, and also because I could see George and his warmongering band of neocons rushing us into a crazy invasion of Iraq, which would create more terrorists.

My premonition came true, and Casey was KIA 04/04/04—a mere five days after his unit arrived in Sadr City, Baghdad: *in combat*. The most troubling thing, though, is, that some recruiters are still promising young people that they won't have to go to Iraq if they sign up. I am being told that all the time by young people who talk to the multi-level marketers working toward their bonuses—oops, I mean military recruiters.

As long as our young people are being lied to and used so dishonorably in an unjust invasion and occupation of another country; as long as they are fighting for a corrupt government and still without the proper equipment, food, training, or leadership; as long as moms are having to hold bake sales to buy their sons' body armor; as long as our soldiers are being held against their wills long after they have done their duty; as long as they are being sent to kill innocent people, military service should be opposed.

Let's affirm life in the fullest for everybody: the unfortunate, uncounted people of Iraq who are "acceptable collateral damage" to the war hawks, and our own indispensable loved ones. The only way to support our troops is to bring them home from this mess—now.

The American public and Congress need to hear more stories from the front. The tragedy and atrocities of this occupation need to be in the forefront of every American's mind, so there can be an uprising of peace. If you have a story similar to the ones I have told, please forward them to me. Representative Dennis Kucinich (D–OH) would like to put these stories, now engraved only in our hearts, into the *Congressional Record.*

WHY AREN'T LIARS HELD TO THE SAME STANDARDS AS THE PEOPLE TRYING TO EXPOSE THEM?

My antiwar, pro-peace stance has put me in contact with so many people all over the world. I believe that my willingness to share my heart and tragic story (and in the process, tell the truth) helps people open up to me in ways that they cannot do with others. In the past few days, I have been bombarded with horror stories about what our government is doing to innocent Americans.

I was driving from one event to another the other day, and I got a call from an Iranian woman who is now a citizen of the United States and who has been in the U.S. for thirty years, is married to an American, and has a five-year-old son and a brother who has been in prison for nine months for wanting to serve America.

My new Iranian-American friend—I will call her Susie since her family is in danger of reprisal—told me that her brother signed up for the National Guard to give something back to the country that he has adopted as his own. He was lied to by his recruiter, who said he could have his student loans paid off and become an American citizen within a year. He also has severe learning disabilities, and his recruiter falsified his test scores and his application. Susie's brother was told that the mistakes would be "corrected" before the application was turned in. Like my KIA son Casey, Susie's brother naïvely trusted his recruiter.

One day, Susie's brother, who was at that time in training to be a chemical specialist, was sitting in class when FBI agents came in and hauled him off to prison. He was told it was because he went to Iran twice after 9/11 (his country of birth and his family's country), and because he falsified his application to get into the National Guard. Susie's brother thought that going into the National Guard was going to be a good and admirable thing, and he was deceived and betrayed. He didn't get his student loans paid off, he didn't get citizenship, but he did get thrown in jail without proper legal representation. Susie called her state's senators to see if they could help her and her brother, and she was told to quit making trouble or her entire family would be investigated.

Then yesterday when I was traveling from event to event again, I got another phone call from a hysterical mom, Summer, whose son was killed in Iraq in April 2005. Her medic son was found face down on his bunk with some morphine bottles around him. Summer was told that he died of a drug overdose, and the report stated that her daughter-in-law and her son's battle buddies all said that he abused drugs in Iraq. Summer was devastated. She knew her boy. She knew her son didn't take drugs. She finally got hold of the reports, and they contradicted what she had been told by the military. All of the people interviewed said her son *did not* abuse drugs. She received the toxicology report two months after her son died, and he *did not* have any drugs in his system. How did Summer's son die, and why is the Army trying to cover it up? Wasn't it bad enough that this government took Summer's son and killed him in an unjust, immoral, and illegal war? They had to lie to her, too?

This past weekend, I spent time at Kevin and Monica Benderman's house at Fort Stewart, Georgia. Kevin, a conscientious objector who refused to go back to Iraq with the Third Infantry Division and kill innocent people and participate in other war crimes, was convicted in his court martial on July 28 of "missing movement" and was sentenced to fifteen months in federal prison. Kevin was obviously made an example to other soldiers who are also thinking of protesting this obscene occupation by refusing to kill blameless people or die themselves. From the testimony that was given by the prosecution at the court martial, it is clear that witnesses lied about Kevin and that documents were falsified. I hate to see a brave, honorable, and patriotic American like Kevin railroaded to federal prison for standing up for what he knows is moral and correct. What makes Kevin's treatment even worse is that those who are responsible for killing and maiming tens of thousands of innocent people and for the destruction of an innocent country are roaming around the world free to unleash more death and pandemonium.

For my effort in trying to awaken America to the dirty tricks and fraud of our government and for trying to call attention to the fact that thousands of people are dying and in harm's way in Iraq for the lies, I am often called a traitor, terrorist supporter, Jane Fonda, unpatriotic, etcetera. I am called names that contain words that good Christian supporters of George should not even know, let alone use. I am accused of not supporting the troops, and people tell me that Casey would be spinning in his grave, on which I am alternately spitting, pissing, or s*itting.

What has happened to America? What has happened to our freedoms? Where did sanity go? Where is the due process that we have always been entitled to? Why do people feel free to castigate the mother of a "war hero" for exercising her freedom of speech, and why does our leadership feel free to lie to mothers of "war heroes"? Why aren't the liars being held to the same standards as the people who are trying to expose them?

Stories like these are becoming more and more common in the USA. The un-Patriot Act and the total disregard for the Constitution by nearly everyone who holds an elected or appointed position in our federal government are starting to hit too close to home for many people. When will the rest of

America finally come out of its coma? When, God forbid, the jack-booted thugs come pounding on their door some midnight?

People like the Bendermans, Summer, Susie, and her brother should be defended and supported by every true American. The injustice of what is happening to some good, hard-working, and honest Americans is overwhelming, unfair, and un-American.

Ben Franklin said, "Those who would sacrifice essential liberties for a little temporary safety deserve neither liberty nor safety." We are rapidly becoming a nation with neither. We should demand both and refuse to give up any of our liberties or our security. These things are our birthrights. Please don't give up yours. I am not giving up mine.

THE SOUNDS OF HOPE

Have you ever heard the sound of a mother screaming
    for her son?
The torrential rains of a mother's weeping will never
    be done.
They call him a hero, you should be glad he's one, but,
Have you ever heard the sound of a mother screaming
    for her son?

Have you ever heard the sound of a father holding
    back his cries?
They say he must be brave because his boy died for
    another man's lies.
The only thing he allows himself are long, deep sighs.
Have you ever heard the sound of a father holding
    back his cries?

Have you ever heard the sound of taps played at your
brother's grave?
They say he died so the flag will continue to wave,
But I believe he died because they had oil to save.
Have you ever heard the sound of taps played at your
brother's grave?

Have you ever heard the sound of a Nation Rocked to
Sleep?
The leaders want to keep you numb so the pain won't
be so deep,
But if we the people let them continue, another mother
will weep.
Have you ever heard the sound of a Nation Rocked to
Sleep?

"A Nation Rocked to Sleep/For Casey"
By Carly Sheehan, © Copyright 2004

The sounds my daughter writes about in this amazing,
inspired poem are imprinted in my DNA. I will never, ever forget the night of April 4, 2004, when I found out that Casey had
been killed. After what seemed an eternity, I finally began to
wonder who or what was making those horrible screaming
noises. Then I realized it was me. It couldn't have been Casey's
father, because he was paralyzed in stunned silence holding the
pair of pants he had been folding when the deliverers of death
news arrived.

I will also never forget the day we buried my sweet boy, my
oldest son. I'll never forget the playing of taps or the violent
and, in hindsight, thoughtless volley of the twenty-one-gun
salute. If I live to be a very old lady and forget everything else,
I will never forget when the general handed me the folded flag
that had lain on Casey's coffin, as his brother and sisters,
standing behind me, sobbed.

The saddest thing about the obscene sounds of violence is that they never should have been heard in the first place. From Maine to California, and from Baghdad to Falluja, these dirges were unnecessary. In my travels, and from hundreds of e-mails, phone calls, cards, and letters, I am discovering that people who formerly supported the invasion of Iraq are withdrawing their support. I even believe that many of our fellow citizens who still support the ignominy of Iraq are doing so because they are clinging to the deceptions so desperately, because they want the deceptions to so be the truth. It will be painful to come to terms with supporting the lies of this administration. It will be painful to know that wholesale killing of innocent people occurred because you and so many others believed the betrayals, but acknowledging the mistake is the first step to correcting it. And, believe me, acknowledging the mistake is not as painful as hearing those devastating sounds.

Representative Walter Jones (R–NC) has realized that he was duped into supporting the invasion. I have spoken to him about his change of heart, and he is so sad that his wholehearted support of the administration helped cause so many good people to hear those gut-wrenching sounds of grief. But he is going forward to do what he can to end this occupation as soon as possible. He has co-sponsored a bipartisan bill (HRJ 55) with other congressional leaders like Dennis Kucinich (D–OH) and Ron Paul (R–TX) to force our administration into a troop withdrawal beginning October 1, 2006. The bill is a good first step toward ensuring that families here in America and all over the world do not have to suffer needless death in war. However, I would like the withdrawal to begin tomorrow, because I don't even want to try and imagine the sounds Casey heard before he died. I don't want to imagine the sound of the bullet strong enough to pierce the Kevlar coating on his helmet to rip through his skull. I don't want to know the sounds of a mother in Iraq wailing for her entire family. These sounds need to stop immediately! It is time to bring our troops home.

The sound I do want to hear is the sound of a Nation Waking Up. I will rejoice to hear the sounds of the collective *mea culpa* and the beating of breasts. I want to hear the deafening clicks as the steady stream of news-o-tainment is turned off, propaganda that is turning us into zombies who are numb to the truth. I want to hear the sound of our children getting off planes and boats from Iraq to the joyful squealing of their children and the deep sighs of relief from their spouses, parents, and other loved ones. I want to hear our citizenry lifting up their voices in chorus and singing, "We will never let this happen again."

II.

LETTERS

I wish I could convey to you in person the pain and devastation your reckless policies have brought to my life. The grief is so profound and primal that it can't easily be described by the written word. You can't see my red, swollen eyes or my grief-etched face. Your policies have created a hole in my heart and in our family that can never be filled.

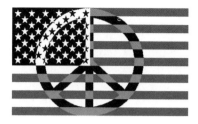

REWARDING INCOMPETENCE

Letter to *Time* Magazine

December 21, 2004

DEAR TIME EDITORS:

My son, Spc. Casey Sheehan, was killed in Iraq on 04/04/04. This has been an extraordinary couple of weeks of "slaps in the faces" to us families of fallen heroes.

First, Secretary of Defense Donald Rumsfeld admits to the world something that we as military families already know: The United States was not prepared for nor had any plan for the assault on Iraq. Our children were sent to fight an ill-conceived and badly prosecuted war. Our troops were sent with the wrong type of training, bad equipment, inferior protection, and thin supply lines. Our children have been killed and we have made the ultimate sacrifice for this fiasco of a war, and then we find out this week that Rumsfeld doesn't even have the courtesy or compassion to sign the "death letters," as they are so callously called. Besides the upcoming holidays and the fact that we miss our children desperately, what else can go wrong this holiday season?

Well let's see. Oh yes. George W. Bush awards the Presidential Medal of Freedom to three more architects of the quagmire that is Iraq. Thousands of people are dead, and

Bremer, Tenet, and Franks are given our country's highest civilian award. What's next?

To top everything off, after it has been proven that Iraq had no weapons of mass destruction, there were no ties between Saddam and 9/11, and over 1300 brave young people in this country are dead and Iraq lies in ruins, what does *Time* magazine do? Names George W. Bush as its "Man of the Year." The person who betrayed this country into a needless war and whom I hold ultimately responsible for my son's death and who was questionably elected, again, to a second term, is honored this way by your magazine.

I hope we finally find peace in our world and that our troops who remain in Iraq are brought home speedily. After all, there was no reason for our troops to be there in the first place. No reason for my son and over 1300 others to have been taken from their families. No reason for the infrastructure of Iraq to be demolished and thousands of Iraqis to be killed. No reason for the notion of a "happy" holiday to be robbed from my family forever. I hope that our "leaders" don't invade any other countries that pose no serious threat to the United States. I hope there is no draft. I hope that the five people mentioned here (and many others) will finally be held responsible for the horrible mistake they got our country into. I hope that competence is finally rewarded and incompetence is appropriately punished. These are my wishes for 2005.

This isn't the first time your magazine has selected a questionable man for this honor, but it's the first time it has affected my family so personally and so sorrowfully.

Sincerely,

CINDY SHEEHAN

YOUR POLICIES HAVE CREATED A HOLE IN MY HEART THAT CAN NEVER BE FILLED

Letter to Donald Rumsfeld

January 9, 2005

TO THE SECRETARY OF DEFENSE:

At a recent news conference, you made a plea for understanding your concern for the lives of U.S. soldiers in Iraq. You said, "I hope and pray that every family member of those who have died so bravely knows how deeply I feel their loss," and that you "stay awake at night for concern for those at risk," and that the grief of our loved ones "is something that I feel to my core."

You claim that you deeply feel our loss, and you are trying to appear very compassionate and caring. It is my feeling since my son, Spc. Casey Austin Sheehan, was killed in Sadr City in an ambush on 04/04/04, that the soldiers who have been sent over there to die for your administration's lies and betrayals are the least of your concerns. If you really cared about our brave young men and women who have been put into harm's way for no reason, you would have brought them home months ago when it was proven that Iraq had no WMDs, no connection with 9/11, when Saddam was captured and the Iraqis were given freedom from him, etcetera. If you cared about our soldiers before the falsehoods were exposed to the light, you would have sent them over to fight a war with the proper planning, training, armor, equipment, and supplies. You would have been more realistic and planned better for the occupation.

Now the big story that you and yours are telling is that America has troops over in Iraq to bring Iraqis democracy and to give them control of their own country. One of our questions for you would be: If this is true, after the sham elections and after you all have your puppet government installed in Iraq, are you going to bring our troops home? After the elections, what's going to be the reason to keep our young people in danger? What's going to be the reason to keep millions of innocent Iraqis in danger?

My son was told that he would be going to Iraq to rebuild schools, sewer systems, and relationships with the people of Iraq. He was lied to, also. He was told that he would be welcomed as a "liberator" with "chocolates and flowers." Well, he was killed two short weeks after he arrived in Iraq, and he wasn't killed by chocolates and flowers. It was RPGs and small arms fire. Since you all have tried to equate Saddam and Osama and make us citizens of the USA believe that they are the same person, are you trying to convince us that chocolates and flowers are the same as grenades and bullets? Using double-speak, are we to believe that "liberator" and "occupier" are one and the same?

Mr. Rumsfeld, you tried these politics of fear in the Ford administration, and you are playing them again with us. I just want to let you know that there are some people who aren't afraid. We are fighting to bring our children home from this illegal and immoral war, and we are fighting to bring peace and democracy back to our country.

There is a group of Gold Star families who are going to be in Washington, D.C., for the Inauguration, between January 19 and January 21. We have requested a meeting with you, and we haven't received one yet. My challenge to you would be for you to meet with us if you care so much for and feel our losses so deeply. It would be an excellent opportunity for you to prove that you have compassion for our children and truly do care about our losses. We, as families, have many other questions for you, also. For example: The DOD still says that my son's death is "under investigation." When I request information, I do not even get a reply. My son was killed due to the lack of proper training, proper armor, proper equipment, and proper planning. Why? Your public answers to questions such as these have been inadequate and very flippant, and instead of bringing peace and assurance to many of us Gold Star families, your statements hurt us more deeply.

In requesting our meeting, we, the families, gave you a deadline to respond to us. That deadline is January 10, 2005. We come from all over the country and we all have numerous media contacts. As I stated last week, if we do not hear from your office regarding this meeting, we are going to the media. I think your attitude about the safety of our troops and lack of compassion for not signing the so-called "death letters" has been a very big news story, and I think the media would be interested to know that you won't meet with us. I think the media would also be interested to know that you will meet with us if a meeting is set up.

Mr. Secretary, in the above quote you stated that you "stay up at night" with concern for those at risk. Well, I haven't had a good night of sleep, free of nightmares, since 04/04/04. My nights are full of grief and my days are full of pain. My family just passed our first Christmas without Casey, and it was so depressing I couldn't even bring myself to get my decorations out. I couldn't bear to see Casey's stocking, which has been hung in joyful anticipation for the past twenty-five years. We just passed the nine-month "anniversary" of his death. He was in my womb for his first nine months, and the past nine months he has been in the womb of our mother earth.

I wish I could convey to you in person the pain and devastation your reckless policies have brought to my life. The grief is so profound and primal that it can't easily be described by the written word. You can't see my red, swollen eyes or my grief-etched face. At this point, I have the feeling that you think that my son was a spendable resource for you, like a bullet or a bomb. But my son was an indispensable part of our family and my heart and soul. Your policies have created a hole in my heart and in our family that can never be filled. Never. I think it is your responsibility to meet with us, and our right as Americans and families of heroes to be granted this meeting. I know it would ease our minds to have the answers to our questions and the assurance that you really do feel our losses deeply. A meeting with us would be a chance to put your words into action. This will be my third and final request.

CINDY SHEEHAN

BUSH IS DEFENDING LIFE?

Letter to White House Spokesperson Dana Perino

March 30, 2005

DEAR MS. PERINO,

I read with great interest and excitement your quote in *The Washington Post* dated March 26, 2005. The article is titled "Bush's Back-and-Forth Reflects Rift in Party." The author, Peter Baker, quotes you as saying, "President Bush supports all those who stand up to defend life."

You don't know how absolutely *thrilled* I was when I read that quote, because *I support life!!* I am so honored that President Bush supports me and my organization!!

My organization, Gold Star Families for Peace, got together specifically to end this war and to end the killing in Iraq. Gold Star Families for Peace is made up of family members who have lost precious loved ones in the invasion/occupation of Iraq. We are opposed to the killing on both sides of the conflict.

Especially the estimated 200,000 innocent Iraqi civilians who have been killed.

Here are some concrete things that President Bush can do to support me and my organization in our life-defending activities:

1) Bring our troops home from Iraq now so no other innocent people have to be killed.

2) Change the $81-billion-killing-and-war-profit appropriations bill into a reparations bill.

3) Stop meddling in the affairs of sovereign Middle Eastern countries like Iran and Syria.

4) Bring members of my organization to the White House to show his support for our life-defending activities. This visit would not have to include any medals. Just a public expression of support for our life-defending activities would be appropriate.

5) Stop misleading the world about the reasons he invaded Iraq and stop misleading the world in his reasons for staying in Iraq.

6) Stop appointing people who support war and torture to high-level positions: Condoleezza Rice, Alberto Gonzales, John Bolton, John Negroponte, Paul Wolfowitz, to name a few.

7) Stop trying to cover up the quagmire of Iraq by going all over the country misleading us about the mess Social Security is in.

8) Take some of the reparations money for Iraq and fully fund the VA and veterans groups to help take care of our physically, mentally, and emotionally wounded children who are coming back barely alive from Iraq themselves.

9) Do not, under any circumstances, attack Iran or Syria.

10) Did I mention, bring our children home from Iraq, now??

I have other ideas, if the president or you would like to contact me or meet with me.

Again, please congratulate the president for supporting activities that defend life. Please let him know that Gold Star Families for Peace is fully behind life and that we are relieved that the situation in Iraq should be coming to a swift end now. We are also joyful that all of our children who come home will now be taken care of the way they deserve. We are also pleased that the Iraqi people will now be able to rebuild their own country and get on with their lives without being occupied.

My hope is restored.

Thank you Mr. President.

HAVE YOU LOST YOUR MINDS?

Letter to Congressmembers

August 3, 2005

DEAR ELECTED OFFICIALS,

When are you all going to take back your constitutional authority from the maniac in the White House? If you all won't protect us, who will?

We are seriously screwed, and you all sit back and let the administrative branch take away our freedoms and foist criminals on us: people with no humanity or regard for our American Constitution or humanity. People like Alberto Gonzales and John Negroponte and most recently, John Bolton—torturers and murderers—to name a few. You in fact are complicit in stealing our freedoms by extending the unconstitutional and unpatriotic Patriot Act. Have you all lost your minds?

CINDY SHEEHAN

III.

SPEECHES

*You cannot put a price on what I have given
to this country. I gave them my oldest son,
and they don't even have the courtesy to reply
to say, "No, we're not going to meet with
you," or, you know, "Maybe later."*

Talk at the Counter-Inauguration Protest

On the Steps of National City Christian Church, Washington, D.C.

January 20, 2005

Hi. I've had a very busy day today. We Gold Star Families for Peace have been trying for weeks to get a meeting with the secretary of defense. We have been e-mailing, writing, and calling. They finally stopped taking our calls. And I just saw all of these people today cheering for them and their policies, and I think, "If I had like twenty-five grand, I would probably have access to everybody in this administration."

But I have paid a price that is priceless. You cannot put a price on what I have given to this country. I gave them my oldest son, and they don't even have the courtesy to reply to us to say, "No, we're not going to meet with you," or, you know, "Maybe later," or "Would you like to meet with another aide?" They don't even have the courtesy to meet with Gold Star Families. I was on *Good Morning, America* this morning, and they asked me why I opposed the inauguration, and I said, "While these people are partying tonight, there's going to be more bloodshed. I just think it's very inappropriate to celebrate when there are millions of people in harm's way."

PEACE RALLY OUTSIDE FORT BRAGG, FAYETTEVILLE, NORTH CAROLINA

Commemorating the Second Anniversary of the Invasion of Iraq

March 19, 2005

I often get introduced as a mother who lost her son in Iraq. I didn't lose Casey. I know right where he is. He is in a grave in Vacaville, and I know who put him there: George Bush and the rest of the arrogant and ignorant neocons in D.C. who murdered my son and tens of thousands of other innocent people. Why are they still in our capital? Why are they still running our country? With state-sponsored terror and sustained torture, we have to face it: we're governed by psychopathic killers who need to go.

For me, today is two anniversaries. One is the second anniversary of the so-called Shock and Awe. It is also the first anniversary of my son's deployment to Iraq. In sixteen days, my family will suffer the one-year death-iversary of Casey. Casey was a brave, honest, loving, kind, and gentle soul who was needlessly and senselessly killed for lies. Since this war is based on lies and betrayals, not one more drop of blood should be spilled, not one more penny for killing. If our Congress votes to give Mr. Bush $81 billion more, they should soak their hands in blood, not ink from sham elections in Iraq. On this day, we should remember the terrible losses of our country that we have suffered and the devastating losses, too, of the Iraqis, especially we families who have paid the terrible price for our leaders' recklessness. I have a challenge for George W. Bush. If we're exporting democracy, why doesn't he march his daughters over there? If he won't send his kids, he should bring our kids home now!

OUR COUNTRY HAS BEEN OVERTAKEN BY MURDEROUS THUGS

Riverside Church, New York

April 4, 2005

My son was killed in Iraq on this day one year ago, the same day of April on which Martin Luther King Jr. was killed in 1968. Dr. King wrote these words from a jail in Birmingham: "We will have to repent in this generation not merely for the hateful words and actions of the bad people but for the appalling silence ... of the good people."

And the Apostle Paul said this:

"[T]hose who desire to be rich fall into temptation ... into a snare that plunges men into ruin and destruction. For the love of money is the root of all evil."

Thirty years ago, 1975, Gerald Ford was president of the United Sates. His chief of staff was Dick Cheney. His secretary of defense was Donald Rumsfeld. Paul Wolfowitz was heading up the international arms-control end of things. All of these positions related directly to national security. While these men were looking after the nation's safety, they and President Ford concluded that Iran needed to supplement its energy system by adding nuclear power. The nuclear energy project that these men approved would have netted certain U.S. corporations billions of dollars. Had the Shah of Iran, a blood-bought servant of U.S. corporate interests, not soon been overthrown by his own countrymen, the bigwigs at Westinghouse or General Electric, or perhaps both, would have amassed personal fortunes from this one project alone.

Some of the stockholders would have also made bundles on the deal.

In 1975, my son had not yet been born. Today he is in his grave. Dick Cheney, on the other hand, is now vice president of the United States, and he is materially wealthy beyond what any of us would ever pray to be. This is the same Dick Cheney who, during the months leading up to the invasion of Iraq, said that Saddam Hussein not only has stockpiles of weapons of mass destruction—more than a hundred metric tons of the deadly stuff—but he also said that Saddam Hussein was well-advanced in developing nuclear weapons and that therefore the U.S. must invade Iraq and dethrone Saddam Hussein. Clean, quick, and simple, according to Dick Cheney. Yet, for some time now, he has changed his tune. He now says, as if he had said it all along, that the U.S. occupation of Iraq will require years of difficult and sometimes-bloody conflict before Iraq is stable enough to bring our loved ones home. And so, rather than speak of weapons of mass destruction, he now uses the word "democracy" a lot.

Is there still an American who cannot clearly see that Dick Cheney, whether in 1975 or 2005, will say whatever he thinks is required to ultimately cause wealth and power to move to himself and to his friends? Need I defile this holy place with words like "Halliburton" and "Kellogg, Brown & Root" and "torture" and "U.S. weapons industry"? Indeed, the Apostle Paul is correct in saying that, ultimately, the love of money leads to ruin and destruction.

Donald Rumsfeld is again secretary of defense. Only yesterday, it seems, he told the whole world that Saddam Hussein has stockpiles of weapons of mass destruction. He even announced to the world that he and his generals knew where Saddam's feared weapons were hidden. He announced this only days before our loved ones risked their lives searching those very areas where he so confidently said the weapons were hidden.

Tell me, isn't it entirely reasonable for us to assume that those very places were being surveilled every second of every day and night until the very moment when our loved ones reached those areas and began their search? Donald Rumsfeld told us that the search would net more than a hundred metric tons. Are we to believe that Saddam quickly assembled a caravan of eighteen-wheelers and loaded all this stuff up and hauled it away to some new hiding place, and that U.S. surveillance, the best in the world, didn't notice any of this happening? Are we to believe that this administration was, once again, asleep at the wheel, just as they would have us believe that they were innocently caught off-guard on the morning of September 11, 2001?

I implore you to read some of Scott Ritter, and you will finally begin to understand that the horrid price we and the people of Iraq have paid to discover that Saddam's weapons of mass destruction had already been destroyed is not the result of any failure at the U.S. intelligence agencies. It is, in fact, a validation of U.S. intelligence agencies. Ritter will explain to you exactly how Rumsfeld was well informed by knowledgeable people within the intelligence community, that Saddam had been stripped clean of such weapons, that Saddam's ability to reconstitute such weapons' programs had also been destroyed, and that any moves Saddam might have made in that direction would have been observed and stopped forthwith.

Is there anyone in America who cannot yet see that Donald Rumsfeld is a liar, that he will say anything so long as he thinks it will help shape the world to his own liking? Is there even one sane adult among us who cannot see that Donald Rumsfeld is a threat to our nation's security and to peace on our beloved earth?

Paul Wolfowitz, after months of not finding any weapons of mass destruction and after hundreds of U.S. soldiers were killed—my son among them—and after tens of thousands of innocent Iraqi citizens were killed, this same Paul Wolfowitz casually explained, with his kindly charade and his ever-so-soft voice, that a decision was made to put forth "weapons of mass destruction" as the need for the invasion. Essentially, Paul Wolfowitz admitted that he and his fellow conspirators had decided among themselves, "Let's just go with the bit about weapons of mass destruction. It's the one thing that will scare the American people enough so as to cause them to get behind this invasion."

As soft-spoken and sincere-sounding as Paul Wolfowitz is, is there yet any sane adult in this country whose skin does not crawl when this murderous liar opens his mouth and speaks? Am I the only person in this room who clearly sees that Paul Wolfowitz is a threat to our nation's security and to peace on our beloved earth?

Thirty years ago these three men gave the green light to Iran so that Iran could hire U.S. companies to go there and build a $6.4 billion nuclear power facility. No doubt the final bill would have been at least three times that much. Yet Dick Cheney recently said this of Iran's current intentions to add nuclear power to its energy system: "They are already sitting on an awful lot of oil and gas. Nobody can figure why they need nuclear to generate energy." Did these men not notice thirty years ago, while they and their cohorts were being wined and dined by the Shah, that the opulent surroundings were bought and paid for with oil and gas that were being taken from the ground beneath their feet? Yet these men agreed, clear back then, that Iran needed to add nuclear power to its energy system. It is now thirty years and God only knows how many tens of millions of barrels of oil later. Why should we believe these men, who we know are liars, when they now say that Iran's primary motive for wanting nuclear power is so that they can make nuclear weapons with which to destroy us and our allies? Even now, the International Atomic Energy Agency reports that there is no evidence that Iran has a nuclear weapons program. The Bush administration's response? They are trying to oust the agency's lead inspector, Mohammed al-Baradei. But who can forget that it was Mr. al-Baradei and the International Atomic Energy Agency who, during the months prior to the invasion of Iraq, reported that Saddam no longer had a nuclear weapons program.

Our country has been overtaken by murderous thugs, gangsters who lust after fortunes and power; never caring that their addictions are at the expense of our loved ones and the blood of innocent people near and far. We've watched these thugs parade themselves before the whole world as if they are courageous advocates for Christian moral values and the spread of democracy. Yet we all know that they are now putting in place, all across this country, a system of voting that provides no way to validate the accuracy of the counting of the votes. Our loved ones have been buried in early graves even as these arrogant thugs parade themselves before the entire world, insisting that democracy is worth dying for, killing for, and destroying entire cities for, all the while they are busy here at home overseeing the emplacement of an electronic voting system that invites fraud at every turn, an electronic vote-counting system that provides no way to validate the votes cast, and that, by its very design, prohibits the recounting of votes.

For these men to not see to it that our own system of voting and vote counting is accurate, understandable, and verifiable, all the while sending our loved ones to kill and to die so as to establish a democracy in some far-away place, is just one more staggering piece of evidence that the U.S. government is now ruled by murderous hypocrites—criminals who should be arrested, charged appropriately, confined behind bars, and then tried in a court of law, not only here in our own country, but also in all the other countries that have suffered their incomprehensible greed. In their secret hiding places, while celebrating newly won fortunes with their fellow brass, these men must surely congratulate themselves with orgies of carnal pleasure as they mock the multitudes who are yet so blind as to mistake them for God's devoted servants. Thank you.

CONGRESSIONAL FORUM
ON THE DOWNING STREET MEMO

Washington, D.C.

June 16, 2005

Thank you, Congressman Conyers. I wish I could say it was an honor to be here today to testify about the effect the Downing Street Memo has had on me and my family. It is an honor that I wish never had to happen. I believe that not any of us should be gathered here today for this reason, as a result of an invasion and occupation that never should have happened.

My son, Spc. Casey Austin Sheehan, was killed in action in Sadr City, Baghdad, on 04/04/04. He was in Iraq for only two weeks before L. Paul Bremer inflamed the Shiite militia into rebellion, which resulted in the deaths of Casey and six other brave soldiers who were tragically killed in an ambush. My friend Bill Mitchell, the father of Sergeant Mike Mitchell who was one of the other soldiers killed that awful day, is here with us today. This is a picture of my son Casey when he was seven months old. It's an enlargement of a picture he carried in his wallet until the day he was killed. He loved this picture of himself. It was returned to us with his personal effects from Iraq. He always sucked on those two fingers.

When he was born, he had a flat face from passing through the birth canal, and we called him Edward G., short for Edward G. Robinson. How many of you have ever seen your child in his or her premature coffin? It is a shocking and very painful sight. The most heartbreaking aspect of seeing Casey lying in his casket for me was that his face was flat again because he had no muscle tone. He looked like he did when he was a baby lying in his bassinet.

The most tragic irony is that if the Downing Street Memo proves to be true, Casey and thousands of people should still be alive. I believed when our leaders invaded Iraq in March 2003— I believed before our leaders invaded Iraq in March 2003, and I am even more convinced now—that this aggression on Iraq was based on a lie of historic proportions and was blatantly unnecessary.

The so-called Downing Street Memo dated July 23, 2002, only confirms what I already suspected: that the leadership of this country rushed us into an illegal invasion of another sovereign country on prefabricated and cherry-picked intelligence. Iraq was no threat to the United States of America, and the devastating sanctions and bombing against Iraq were working. As a matter of fact, in interviews in 1999 with respected journalist and long-time Bush family friend, Mickey Herskowitz, then-governor George Bush stated, "One of the keys to being seen as a great leader is to be seen as commander-in-chief. My father had all this political capital built up when he drove the Iraqis out of Kuwait, and he wasted it. If I have a chance to invade, if I had that much capital, I'm not going to waste it. I'm going to get everything passed that I want to get passed, and I'm going to have a successful presidency."

It looks like George Bush was ready to lead this country into an avoidable war even before he became president. From the exposing of the Downing Street Memo and the conversations with George Bush from 1999, it seems like the invasion of Iraq and the deaths of so many innocent people were preordained. It appears that my boy Casey was given a death sentence even before he joined the Army in May 2000.

When a president lies to Congress and the American people, it is a serious offense. If the Downing Street Memo proves to be true, then it would appear that the president, vice president, and many members of the cabinet deceived the world before the invasion of Iraq. As a result of this alleged lie, over 1700 brave young Americans who were only trying to do their duties have come home in flag-draped coffins, images as if they were ashamed of our children that our leaders won't even let the American public see. Thousands upon thousands of Iraqis who were guilty only of the crime of living in Iraq are dead. Thousands of our young people will go through the rest of their lives missing one or more limbs, and too many will come home missing parts of their souls and humanity.

Kevin Lucey, who found his Marine son Jeffrey, who was recently home from Iraq, hanging dead from a garden hose in his basement, wrote to me, "We ask daily where was the urgency? Where was the necessity of rushing in? Can anyone explain to us, his mother and father, why he felt he had to die by his own hand? Why are the ones in position of power so afraid to ask people like us to discuss what happened to Jeff? Jeff can teach us so much. This war was so misguided and had so many other agendas which had nothing to do with the country."

Kevin, who cradled his son when he was his sweet baby boy, cradled Jeff's lifeless body for the last time in his arms after he cut him down from the hose. The Jeff that the Luceys saw march off to a reckless war was not the one who went home. The Jeff his family knew died in Iraq, murdered by the inhumanity of gratuitous war.

The deceptions of the trails that led to the U.S. invasion and occupation of Iraq cost my family a price too dear to pay and almost too much to bear, the precious life of Casey. Casey was a good soldier who loved his family, his community, his country, and his God. He was trustworthy and trusting, and the leadership of his country seemingly betrayed him. He was an indispensable part of our family, an obedient, sweet, funny, and loving son to myself and his father, Pat, an adored big brother to his sisters Carly and Jane and his brother Andy, and the beloved nephew to my sister Auntie, who is here with me today. Our family has been devastated and torn asunder by his murder.

I believe that the reasons that we citizens of the United States of America were given for the invasion of Iraq have unequivocally been proven to be false. I also believe that Casey and his buddies have been killed to line the pockets of already-wealthy people and to feed the insatiable war machine that has always devoured our young. Casey died saving his buddies, and I know so many of our brave young soldiers die doing the same thing. But he and his fellow members of the military should never have been sent to Iraq.

I know the family of Sergeant Sherwood Baker who was killed guarding a team that was looking for the mythical WMDs in Baghdad, the same WMDs that were the justification for invading Iraq as outlined in the Downing Street Memo. Sherwood's brother, Dante Zappala, and his dad, Al Zappala, are here with us today. I believe the Downing Street Memo proves that our leaders betrayed too many innocents into an early grave. The lives of the ones left behind are shattered almost beyond repair.

I also believe an investigation into the Downing Street Memo is completely warranted and a necessary first step toward righting the wrong that is Iraq, and holding someone accountable for the needless, senseless, and avoidable deaths of many thousands. As far as I am concerned, it doesn't matter if one is a Democrat or a Republican—a full investigation into the veracity of the Downing Street Memo must be initiated immediately.

Casey was not asked his political affiliation before he was sent to die in Iraq. The innocent that are having their blood shed by the bucketful in Iraq don't even know or care what American partisan politicking is all about. Every minute that we waste in gathering signatures on petitions or arguing about partisan politics, more blood is being spilled in Iraq. How many more families here in America are going to get the visit from the Grim Reaper dressed in a U.S. military uniform while we are trying to get our congressional leadership to do their duties to the Constitution and to the people of America?

I believe that Congress expediently abrogated their constitutional responsibility to declare war when they passed the War Powers Act, and they bear at least some responsibility for the needless heartache brought on this world by our government. I believe that supporting a full investigation into the Downing Street Memo is a good beginning for Congress to redeem itself for abandoning the Constitution and the American people.

There are too many stories of heartache and loss to tell at a hearing like this. I have testimonies from other families who have been devastated by the war. Their soldiers' names are Sergeant Sherwood Baker, killed in action 04/26/04, First Lieutenant Neil Santoriello, killed in action 08/13/04, Sergeant Mike Mitchell, killed in action 04/04/04, Specialist Casey Sheehan, also killed in action 04/04/04, Lieutenant Jeff Taylor, killed in action 04/07/03, Specialist Kevin Russell, killed in action 04/19/05, Specialist Jonathan Castro, killed in action 12/21/04, Private First Class William Pritchard, killed in action 02/11/04, Specialist Joseph Blickenstaff, killed in action 12/08/03, and First Lieutenant Kenneth Ballard, killed in action 05/30/04. I would like the testimony of these families put into the record and recorded for all to read the words of boundless love, bottomless loss, and deep despair.

There are a few people around the U.S. and a couple of my fellow witnesses who are justifiably a little worried that in my anger and anguish over Casey's premeditated death, I would use some swear words as I have been known to do on occasion when speaking about the subject. Mr. Conyers, out of my deep respect for you, the other representatives here, my fellow witnesses, and viewers of these historic proceedings, I was able to make it through an entire testimony without using any profanity.

However, if anyone deserves to be angry and use profanity, it is I. What happened to Casey and humanity because of the apparent dearth of honesty in our country's leadership is profane, and it defies even my vocabulary skills. We as Americans should be offended more by the profanity of the actions of this administration than by swear words. We have all heard the old adage that actions speak louder than words, and for the sake of Casey and our other precious children, please hold someone accountable for their actions and their words of deception.

Again I would like to thank you for inviting me to testify today and giving me a chance to tell my story, which is the tragic story of too many families here in the U.S. and in Iraq. I hope and pray that this is the first step in exposing the lies to the light and bringing justice for the ones who can no longer speak for themselves. More important, I hope this is a step in bringing our other children home from Iraq. Thank you.

ADDRESS TO
VETERANS FOR PEACE
CONVENTION

Dallas, Texas

August 5, 2005

It's so great to be here.

I got an e-mail yesterday from a man who said, "Cindy, I read everything you write, and I get tears in my eyes. But today I cried real tears, and I screamed, because my dear sweet nineteen-year-old cousin was killed in Iraq." And he said, "Cindy, why didn't I save him? Why didn't I knock him out and take him to Canada?" And I wrote back and said, "You know, we all think that."

I asked my son not to go. I said, "You know it's wrong. You know you're going over there. You know your unit might have to kill innocent people. You know you might die." And he said, "My buddies are going. I have to go. If I don't go, someone's going to have to do my job, and my buddies will be in danger."

What really gets me is these chicken hawks who sent our kids to die without ever serving in a war themselves; they don't know what it's all about. Thirty of our bravest young men have already died this month, and it's only the 5th of August. And the tragedy of the marines from Ohio is awful.

Back in March when we were having our second-year anniversary of the invasion of Iraq, which was pre-empted by Terry Schiavo, so that's all that was on the news, not the more than 4000 of us protesting at Fort Bragg in Fayetteville, North Carolina–Wolf Blitzer said it was insignificant–I wrote an article called "The Amazing Hypocrites," and I asked, why does Terry Schiavo deserve life more than my son and the Iraqi people and the other people that this war has killed.

But do you think George Bush will interrupt his vacation and go visit the families of those twenty marines from Ohio who died this week? No, because he doesn't care. That's not enough to stop his "playing-cowboy" game in Crawford for five weeks.

As you can imagine, to a grieving parent who lost—I don't like to use that word—whose child was murdered, it's extremely difficult, it's an open wound. You can't even get a small scab on that wound, because every day it rips open. I don't know why I do it, because I already know that war is ugly, I already know that war is hard, but every day I open up the Department of Defense website to see who became an angel while I was sleeping. And it rips my heart open again, because I know there is another mother whose life is going to be ruined that day. We can't even begin to heal.

George Bush was speaking after the tragedy of the marines in Ohio, and he said a couple things that outraged me. He never mentioned the terrible incident of those marines, but he did say that the families of the ones who have been killed can rest assured that their loved ones died for a noble cause. And he also said—he says this often and it really drives me crazy— that we have to stay in Iraq and complete the mission to honor the sacrifices of the ones who have fallen.

Why should I want one more mother to go through what I've gone through? The only way he can honor my son's sacrifice is to bring the rest of the troops home, to make my son's death count for peace and love and not war and hatred. I don't want him using my son's death or my family's sacrifice to continue the killing. I don't want him to exploit the honor of my son and others to continue the killing. They sent these honorable people to die and are so dishonorable themselves.

I was writing an e-mail to everybody, and I was so mad, and I just had this brainstorm: I'm going to Dallas to give this speech, so why not go to Crawford afterward and tell him that a Gold Star Mother, somebody whose blood is on his hands, has some questions for him.

I'm going to say, "Listen here, George. Number one, you quit. And I demand, every time you get out there and say that you're going to continue the killing in Iraq to honor the fallen heroes, you say, 'except Casey Sheehan.' And you say, 'Except for all the members of Gold Star Families for Peace,' because we think that not one drop of blood should be spilled in our families' names. Quit doing that. You don't have my permission."

And I'm going to say, "And tell me what 'noble cause' my son died for." And if he even starts to say "freedom and democracy," I'm going to say, "Bullshit. You tell me the truth. You tell me that my son died for oil. You tell me that my son died to make your friends rich. You tell me that my son died to spread the cancer of Pax Americana, imperialism in the Middle East. You tell me that. Don't tell me my son died for freedom and democracy. Because we're not freer. You're taking away our freedoms. The Iraqi people aren't freer; they're much worse off than before you meddled in their country. You get America out of Iraq. And you get Israel out of Palestine."

I had this idea, and I thought it was going to be just my sister and me driving to Crawford, but it kind of mushroomed and people from as far away as Dayton, Ohio, are coming to help us, to stand behind us. I travel all over the country to speak. And I write and get feedback on my writing, and just in the little over a year that I've been doing this, I've seen a major turnaround in this country. People don't just want to hear it; they want to know what they can do.

We have to have everybody impeached that lied to the American public—the executive branch and anyone in

Congress, and all the way down. And we can't let somebody rise to the top who will pardon these war criminals. They need to go to prison for what they've done in this world.

So, anyway, I'm going to go to Crawford tomorrow, and I'm going to say I want to talk to him. And when they say he's not coming out, I'm going to set up my tent there until he comes out to talk to me. I have the whole month of August off, just like him. It's just the way it worked out. I was supposed to go to England tomorrow to do some Downing Street things, but Congressman Conyers canceled, so I have a lot of free time on my hands. And if he quits his vacation and goes to D.C., I'll pull up my tent and go to D.C. and put it on the White House lawn, and I'll be waiting for you guys when you get there September 24.

Another thing I'm doing is not paying my taxes for 2004. My son was killed in 2004. If I get a letter from the IRS, I'm going to say, "You know what, this war is illegal," and I'll explain why this war is illegal. "This war is immoral," and I'll explain why this war is immoral. "You killed my son for this. I don't owe you anything. If I live to be a million, I won't owe you a penny. I've paid enough!"

I want them to come after me. I want to put this war on trial. I want to say, "You give me my son, and I'll pay your taxes." Camilo Mejia knew what was right, and he went to prison for it. Henry David Thoreau refused to pay his poll tax, and he went to prison. When Ralph Waldo Emerson came to visit Thoreau and asked, "What are you doing here?" Thoreau responded, "Why aren't you here? This is the only place for a moral person in an immoral world."

It's up to us, the people, to break immoral laws and resist. As soon as the leaders of a country lie to you, they have no authority over you. These maniacs have no authority over us. They might be able to put our bodies in prison, but they can't put our spirits in prison. Camilo came out a much stronger person. He's one of my heroes.

Why do we keep doing this to each other? Why do we let this continue time and time again? Our country is so good at demonizing people. I have relatives from World War II who still call Japanese people "Japs." And we demonize the Iraqi people. Most of this country doesn't even think we're killing innocent people. "Oh Cindy, don't you remember what happened on September 11?" "Yes, but were any of the people who flew planes into the World Trade Center from Iraq?" When I was growing up, it was Communists. Now it's Terrorists. You always have to have somebody to fight and be afraid of, so the war machine can build more bombs, guns, and bullets.

But I do see hope. Fifty-eight percent of the American public is with us. We're preaching to the choir, but the choir's not singing. If all of the 58 percent started singing, this war would end.

I got an e-mail the other day, and it said, "Cindy, if you didn't use so much profanity, there are people on the fence that get offended." And I said, "How in the world is anybody still sitting on that fence? If you fall on the side that is pro-George and pro-war, get your ass over to Iraq and take the place of somebody who wants to come home. And if you fall on the side that is against this war and against George Bush, stand up and speak out. But whatever side you fall on, quit being on the fence."

The opposite of good is not evil. It's apathy. We have to get the people of this country off their butts and get the choir singing. We need to say, "Bring our troops home now!" We can't depend on the people in charge bringing our troops home, because you don't plan on bringing the troops home when you drop so much of the reconstruction money into building permanent bases.

I was hoping to come to your banquet tomorrow night, but unless George comes out and talks to me, I'll be camping at Crawford. Thank you.

IV.

THE PEACEFUL OCCUPATION OF CRAWFORD, TEXAS

August 6–31, 2005

George Bush and his advisers "misunderestimated" me when they thought they could intimidate me into leaving before I had answers. If it shortens the war by a minute or saves one life, it is worth it. This is George Bush's accountability moment, and he is failing miserably.

WHAT NOBLE CAUSE?

Camp Casey, Saturday, August 6

Today we went into the belly of the beast in Crawford, Texas, and lived to tell about it.

On Wednesday, August 3, I had a brainstorm. I was so furious about the horrible loss of life, especially from the Marine National Guard unit from Ohio. I was also so heart-broken for the families who have been wrongfully left behind. Then to top off the indignity and profanity of the needless deaths, George Bush spoke out after the deaths and said two things that enraged me further: "The families of the fallen can rest assured that your loved ones died for a noble cause," and "We have to honor the sacrifices of the fallen by completing the mission."

The first statement is so blatantly false that it angered me for a couple of reasons. First of all, what is the noble cause? The cause changes at will when the previous cause has been proven a lie. Second, because many people in America, when they hear such drivel, allow themselves to be "assured," a lot of people heard that falsehood and said, "Whew, fourteen Marines in one incident, that's bad, but the president said they died for a noble cause. We can get on with our consumering now."

George Bush has spewed the second filth many times, and each time it upsets me more. As a mother, why would I want any other mother—American or Iraqi—to go through the same pain that I am suffering through? My son Casey was an honorable man filled with an integrity rarely seen these days. I am sure that he would be appalled that George uses his death to justify continued killing. I am appalled that George exploits the senseless sacrifice of my family to justify his murderous policies in the Middle East. Also, does it bother anyone else that this man can take a five-week vacation when our soldiers are suffering, dying, and being maimed in Iraq? When innocent Iraqi people are being murdered every day? When I will never be able to fully enjoy another vacation for the rest of my life?

I was so full of rage and feeling so helpless and like such a failure after all the work for peace that I have done. I was typing an e-mail venting my rage when I had a brainstorm: I am going to Dallas for the Veterans for Peace convention. Why don't I travel up to Crawford and confront George Bush? Why don't I go and demand answers to my questions? I deserve answers to my questions; it is George's moral obligation as the man who is responsible for my son's death to see me. (Please, no e-mails telling me that he has no morals. I know that.) What did Casey and over 100,000 other wonderful human beings die for? What exactly is, George, the "noble cause"? And I demand that you stop using my son's name and my family's sacrifice to continue your illegal and immoral occupation of Iraq.

After I wrote this piece of inspired and impassioned prose, I put my contacts into the e-mail address line and pressed "Send." That's how the peaceful occupation of Crawford, Texas, began.

We convoyed up to Crawford from the Veterans for Peace convention yesterday morning. We had the Impeachment Tour Bus filled with twelve people. We had representatives on the bus from Veterans for Peace, Iraq Veterans Against the War, Vietnam Veterans Against the War, and Gold Star Families for Peace. By the time we got out near Bush's vacation home, we had about forty cars following us.

The details of what we went through when we got to Crawford have been well blogged. From having to walk in a ditch, to being blocked by the county sheriff's department for walking on the road, to the deputy chief of staff and George's personal national security advisor coming out to try and b.s. us into submission, to the Secret Service continuously warning our overnight group that we were going to get run over and killed during the night.

After the initial action of trying to walk up to the ranch, we all went down to a shady place to set up our camp. We were trying to think of a name for our temporary home, when one of the men in Iraq Veterans Against the War suggested "Camp Casey." So in honor of our fallen heroes, we dedicated the camp to the brave men and women who have had their lives ripped away from them by the greedy and power-hungry people who rule our country.

The dozens of people who came out to support Gold Star Families for Peace and the dozen or so who spent the night with me last night would like to tell America a few things:

We are not giving up until George talks to us.

We are humbled and grateful for the support and love we are getting from all over the world.

The beginning of the end of the occupation of Iraq was on August 6, 2005, in, of all places, Crawford, Texas.

DAY THREE

IT IS FREAKIN' AMAZING

Camp Casey, Monday, August 8

Where do I begin? Today was a highly eventful day. This entry won't be artful, but utilitarian. Conservatively, I got three to five phone calls a minute. I did about twenty-five phone interviews and several TV interviews. I did several right-wing radio interviews. I was supposed to do *The Today Show*, an MSNBC live interview, *Connected Coast to Coast* (MSNBC), and *Hardball* (MSNBC). *The Today Show* just never showed up, and the other three MSNBC shows canceled for no reason. Could it be because NBC is owned by General Electric, a major defense contractor??

Another big story that was going on today was about my first meeting with Bush in June of 2004. For you all, I would like to clarify a few things. First of all, I did meet with George, and that is not a secret. I have written about it and been interviewed about it. I will stand by my recounting of the meeting. His behavior was rude and inappropriate. My behavior in June of 2004 is irrelevant to what is going on in 2005. I was in deep shock and deep grief. The grief is still there, but the shock has worn off, and deep anger has set in. And to remind everybody, a few things have happened since June of 2004: the 9/11 Commission Report; the Senate's report on prewar intelligence; the Duelfer WMD report; and, most damaging and criminal, the Downing Street Memo. *The very last thing I have to say about this:* Why do the right-wing media so assiduously scrutinize the words of a grief-filled mother and ignore the words of a lying president?

In the early afternoon, we got word that if we were still there by Thursday, we were going to be deemed a "security threat" to the president. Condi and Rummy are coming in on Thursday for a "policy" meeting. Don't they mean conspiracy-to-commit-crimes meeting? I just don't understand why we will be a security threat on Thursday when we aren't now. If we don't leave on Thursday, will we be arrested? Well, I am not leaving. There are only three things that would make me leave: if George comes out and talks to me, if August comes to an end, or if I am arrested.

People are heading here from all over the country. I have some more Gold Star Families for Peace members coming tomorrow. We are amazed by the outpouring of love and support we are getting. If you can come, then come. Sixty-two percent of the American public are against this war and want our troops home. We need to show the media that we are in the majority. We need to show George Bush and his evil cabal of neocons that when we say, "Bring the troops home, now," we mean, "Bring the troops home, now!!!"

In the late afternoon, many of us left to go back to the Peace House in Crawford, because there was going to be a major lightning storm. While most of us were gone, the sheriff came and told us that what we had been told was county property was really private property and we would have to move our stuff to a tiny place or get it confiscated. I find it interesting that the county sheriff did not know that roads in his county that lead up to the presidential vacation home are private roads. I find it very hard to believe. The bastards think that they are pushing us off, but we will not leave there voluntarily or without handcuffs on. My only hope is that there will be tons of media there when they carry me to the squad car.

Today was so bizarre for me. I got phone calls from famous people pledging their support, and phone calls from mothers with sons in Iraq who are overcome with emotion when they talk to me. And it is so brave for them to call me, because I am their worst fear. We had a young man who is in the U.S. Army at Fort Hood come this morning and spend hours with us. He has been there and his unit is scheduled to go back in October. How much courage did that take for him to come within earshot of his commander-in-chief's home and spend time with some old hippy protestors???

We have a lawyer working on getting us closer and working on magically turning the private property back into county property again. I have some awesome young ladies from Code Pink answering my phone and taking phone calls. We have Veterans for Peace out there putting up banners (our tiny campsite looks really nice). We have concerned citizens from all over America starting to come in. *It is freakin' amazing folks!!!*

Come and join us and let your voices be joined with ours. *Amen!!!*

DAY FOUR

DOGGING GEORGE

Camp Casey, Tuesday, August 9

Today started at 4 a.m. when I had to get up and get ready to be on *Good Morning America*. It was pouring down rain at Camp Casey. The wind was blowing and there was thunder and lightning. It was pretty exciting. The interview went very well. I haven't seen it or read a transcript. Since it was taped, I am just wondering if they showed it when I said Bush doesn't want to see me because he likes to surround himself with "sycophants." I also interviewed with Randi Rhodes, Ed Schultz, Greta Van Susteren, and many others, and closed out the day with my pal Mike Malloy.

The "first meeting" controversy died down a little today

when my town's newspaper printed an op-ed that contradicted Matt Drudge's cherry-picked account of my first meeting with George.

But since they don't have that controversy, they apparently have been lying about other things. Bill O'Reilly said that I am doing this because I have been bought out by "The Arab Anti-Discrimination League." He was telling his viewers that I am a tool for the liberals and that I am a tool for the antiwar movement. Right now, what we are doing right here in Crawford *is* the antiwar movement. We have such a strong coalition of groups: Gold Star Families for Peace, Code Pink, Veterans for Peace, Military Families Speak Out, and the Crawford Peace House.

I talked with John Conyers today, and he wrote a letter to George signed by other Congressmembers to request that George meet with me (see page 80). I also talked to Maxine Waters tonight, and she is probably going to be here tomorrow. I am so overwhelmed by the support.

I did nonstop interviews today. One hundred people came through today to visit with us. About twenty-five people are staying the night. More food, water, flowers, and money came through today. One father brought his two- and four-year-old sons out to meet me and thank me for trying to save his boys from the same fate Casey suffered.

Celeste and Dante Zappala from Philadelphia and Bill Mitchell from Atascadero, California, all members of Gold Star Families for Peace, came out today to support me and help me do interviews and greet all of the people who are arriving.

There is a huge action tomorrow in Aurora, Illinois. George Bush is leaving the ranch tomorrow to go to Aurora to sign a part of the energy bill at the Caterpillar factory. True Majority has raised money to dog George Bush when he leaves the ranch. Every time he leaves, there will be a Gold Star Families for Peace member, Military Families Speak Out members, Veterans for Peace members, and Code Pink members who will protest him and say, "Meet with Cindy." We will not let him have a five-week, nice vacation when there are millions of people in harm's way in Iraq due to his careless policies. The people of Iraq and our soldiers are suffering. Why should George have a nice vacation?

Thank you for all your support and interest. We are making a difference. Keep up the good work.

DAY FIVE

THE TRUTH SCARES PEOPLE

Camp Casey, Wednesday, August 10

Today started at 4 a.m. when the rain started blowing into my tent and my head and my feet started getting soaked and the thunder and lightning came over my tent. I was really frightened for my life, so I abandoned ship and went into Crawford.

By the time we made our way through the floods and got into Crawford, I had a fever, sore throat, and bad headache. So I was made to rest and not have any interviews until noon.

We had a little bit of trouble with locals today. We are beginning to feel a little unwelcome here. One lady almost ran over a film crew that was filming a commercial today. She screamed at us that the neighbors are really mad at us, so we moved down the road to our closest neighbor who is very sweet. Her husband is a medic who just got home from Iraq.

Again, I did tons of interviews. It looks like I will be on the cover of *People* magazine. *Time, Vanity Fair,* and Oprah's magazine will be interviewing me, also.

It was great having the other Gold Star Families for Peace and Military Families Speak Out there to help me with interviews and greeting all of the hundreds of people who came out from all over the country to be with us today. We were hassled by the sheriff because there were too many cars out there. Our little Bush Town has grown to full capacity. The town sheriff said we can put up tents and RVs in the town stadium. There are wall-to-wall sleeping bags here at the Peace House.

Due to the generosity of you all, the Crawford Peace House has gotten over $30,000, and Gold Star Families for Peace has gotten a lot of donations, too. I got about two-and-a-half dozen bouquets of flowers from all over everywhere. I am so amazed and overwhelmed by the support and love we are getting from everywhere.

As for Bill O'Reilly, Sean Hannity, Michelle Malkin, Matt Drudge, etcetera, nothing you can say can hurt me or make me stop what we are doing. We are working for peace with justice. We are using peaceful means and the truth to do it. I guess the truth frightens people. It frightens them so much, they have to resort to telling lies to rebut my arguments. They are despicable human beings and not even worth our concern. Bill O'Reilly had the nerve to invite me on his show again today. But Dolores Kesterson, another Gold Star Families for Peace member who also had a terrible experience with meeting George, was on O'Reilly's show, and she kicked his butt.

Tonight we are still on arrest alert, so we shall see.

Peace soon.

August 10, 2005

The President
The White House
Washington, DC

Dear Mr. President:

We write to respectfully urge you to meet with Cindy Sheehan and other relatives of fallen soldiers who request a meeting to discuss their deep concerns about the war in Iraq. We also request that you help ensure that Ms. Sheehan and her colleagues are not arrested as long as they continue to wait for a meeting with you at their location in the peaceable and legal manner that they have maintained thus far.

Since the loss of her son, Ms. Sheehan and other families have been committed to helping family members of other soldiers who have been lost in Iraq. Ms. Sheehan, in fact, founded Gold Star Families for Peace, a support organization for families of fallen soldiers. For several days now, she has been waiting outside your ranch, hoping to meet with you about the loss of her son and the failure to discover weapons of mass destruction in Iraq. Ms. Sheehan has indicated that she is planning to continue her vigil for the entirety of your vacation at your Crawford complex if necessary.

Given the recent tragic loss of American lives in Iraq, and the many deaths and injuries American troops have sustained since the beginning of the war, we hope that you can appreciate why the family members believe it so important that they exercise their rights as citizens to petition their government. We believe it would send an unfortunate message to other relatives and soldiers if grieving parents were arrested while exercising their constitutional rights.

Thank you very much for you assistance with this matter. We hope that you will be able to make time to meet with Ms. Sheehan and her colleagues and also ensure they are treated fairly while awaiting this important appointment.

Sincerely,

[And 32 other members of Congress]

80

DAY SIX

HOW CAN YOU SPREAD PEACE BY KILLING PEOPLE?

Camp Casey, Thursday, August 11

Day Six of the Peaceful Occupation of Crawford began early this morning when people in cars drove by our camp a few times and blasted on their horns. I just assume they were blaring their approval of us.

Before we get to the less-than-negative things that are happening out at Camp Casey and in the world at large today, over seven hundred people showed up at the camp today. There were more people, flowers, cards, mail, interviews, laughter, heartache, camaraderie, excitement, and just sheer work.

We had the first birthday party tonight at our little event. Alicia from Austin turned seventeen today, and she and her family came to Crawford to celebrate with a cake. Alicia said that she wanted to be out here for her birthday. So many great people from so many parts of the country and our world are here.

Today is kind of a blur to me. From running around from interview to interview, to getting a visit from Viggo Mortensen, today was a whirlwind of activity. I have discovered that the White House press corps is always looking for something to do and someone to cover. We have been happy to oblige them. We had a press conference today with Gold Star Families for Peace and Military Families Speak Out members. It was very effective when people who actually have skin in the game ask the president to be held accountable for the words he has actually said.

Still putting out the O'Reilly fires about my being a traitor and using Casey's name dishonorably. My in-laws sent out a press release disagreeing with me in strong terms, which is totally okay with me, because they barely knew Casey. We have always been on separate sides of the fence politically, and I have not spoken to them since the elections, when they supported the man who is responsible for Casey's death. The thing that matters to me is that my family, Casey's dad and my other three kids, are on the same side of the fence that I am.

Since Congress is not holding George Bush accountable and the media is not doing its job and holding George Bush accountable, we the American people need to hold him accountable for lying to us to get us into a disastrous war. We are finished allowing him to get away with deceiving the American public and abusing his power.

The president says he feels compassion for me, but the best way to show that compassion is by meeting with me and the other mothers and families who are here. Our sons made the ultimate sacrifice, and we want answers. All we're asking is that he sacrifice an hour out of his five-week vacation to talk to us, before the next mother loses her son in Iraq. He says he is spreading peace. How can you spread peace by killing people?

DAY SEVEN

WE HAVE THE POWER

Camp Casey, Friday, August 12

My day started way too early today. After three hours of sleep, I was being shaken awake by someone at 6:30 a.m. telling me that *The Today Show* wanted me to be on their show. I had come into town to sleep in a trailer because my tent had been infested with fire ants. I turned *The Today Show* down for 7:15 a.m., so we did it at 9:00 a.m.

We had a very interesting day. We had Bush drive by really, really fast twice. I caught a glimpse of Laura. I was hoping after she saw me that she would come down to Camp Casey with some brownies and lemonade. I waited for her, but she never came.

The Bushes were going to a barbeque/fundraiser down the road from us. I was very surprised that they let us stay so close to Bush. The families of the fallen loved ones each held their son's cross from Arlington West while Bush drove by. I bet it didn't even give him indigestion to see so many people protesting his murderous policies.

I am a continuing thorn in the side to the right-wing bloggers and right-wing, nut journalists. One man, Phil Hendry, called me an ignorant cow. But you know what? The people who have come out from all over the country to give me a hug and take a picture with me and to support the cause of peace overwhelm me so much, I don't have time to worry about the negativity and the hatred. The people who are slamming me have no idea about what it feels like to unjustly have a child killed in an insane war. Plus, they have no truth to fight truth with, so they fight truth with more lies and hate.

Three active-duty soldiers from Fort Hood came to visit and tell me that they really appreciate what I am doing and that if they were killed in the war, their moms would be doing the same thing. That made me feel so good after all of the negativity I had been hearing from the righties. I also got to hold a couple of toddlers on my lap while their moms or dads took pictures of us. I am honored that people have resonated with the action that I took to make our mission of ending the war a reality.

We are here at the Crawford Peace House now, and there are dozens and dozens of people here. We are giving each other hugs and kisses, and we are all feeling great, full of energy and so filled with hope that this is something that is really going to change the world. I came here so angry, and I have been so encouraged and overwhelmed by the support from all over. I was thinking that there is no reason for us progressive liberals to be angry anymore. We have the power. One mom has shown that we can be the change in our government. We deserve to hold George Bush accountable—no one else does. We have to make sure he answers to us. If he doesn't have to answer to Congress, or the media, we will *force* him to answer to us. I am astonished by the absolute hubris of the person who won't!

DAY EIGHT

HOPE IS BLOSSOMING

Camp Casey, Saturday, August 13

It is not often that Cindy Sheehan is at a loss for words. I will try and describe today, though. It was the most incredible, fantastic, fabulous, amazing, powerful, miraculous event I have ever been a part of. I was so humbled and honored at the outpouring of love and support that arrived in Camp Casey today.

It was a busy morning of interviews and problem solving. I had interviews with some network shows and a photo shoot for the *Vanity Fair* article. Almost all of the reporters ask me if I have accomplished anything at Camp Casey, and I think we really have. We have brought the war onto the front pages of the newspapers and the top stories of the mainstream media. It is really incredible that we are doing so well in the media, because I keep

Following a rally in Crawford, Texas, car after car caravans to Camp Casey. "It was miraculous, like Field of Dreams. *We are building a movement, and they are coming."*

Casey's second Christmas, 1980.
Casey, Mom and Dad, 2000.
The Sheehan kids, Summer 1998:
Janey, Carly, Andy, and Casey.

TOP: *Volunteers place crosses in memory of soldiers killed in Iraq.*

Cindy reflects after placing Casey's boots at the cross bearing his name.

ABOVE: *In memory of Ken Ballard.*

TOP LEFT: *Joan Baez performs at Camp Casey II.*

TOP CENTER: *Big tent at Camp Casey II, with "Arlington Texas" in front. Each cross represents an American soldier killed in Iraq.*

ABOVE LEFT: *Displeased rancher.*

ABOVE CENTER: *Gold Star Families for Peace.*

ABOVE: *Grief and mutual support at Camp Casey.*

BELOW: *"Reverend Al Sharpton gave an amazing talk in support of Camp Casey and all we are doing."*

ABOVE: *Banner honoring Casey at Camp Casey II.*

RIGHT: *Cindy with Ruben Flores, whose son was killed in Iraq in June. "Every time I meet a Gold Star parent whose child died after Casey, it is like a stab in my heart."*

BELOW: *Morning press conference at Camp Casey.*

TOP: Cindy with Tomas Young, who was wounded in Iraq the same day Casey was killed, and other members of Iraq Veterans for Peace.

LEFT: Veteran honors fallen soldiers.

ABOVE: Cindy boards Bring Them Home Now Tour bus, going from Camp Casey to Washington, D.C.

ABOVE: *Cindy waves as she begins speech to 300,000 antiwar protestors in Washington, D.C.*

BELOW: *Cindy is arrested outside the White House gate, "protesting the tragic and needless deaths of tens of thousands of innocent Iraqis and Americans."*

telling all of the reporters that I am doing their jobs. I am asking the tough questions of the president that they don't ask.

We are also gathering people together in this country who believe that this war is a mistake and our troops should come home. I know people have been frustrated, either sitting on the fence or apathetically sitting on the sidelines. Before Casey was killed, I didn't think that one person could ever make a difference in the world. Now I know that isn't true. Not only can one person make a difference, but one person, with millions behind her, can make history. I really believe that this movement that began in Crawford, Texas (does the irony escape anyone?), is going to grow and grow and transform the world. Like I said last night in my blog: hope is blossoming in Crawford, because *we* have the power.

The CBS reporter whom I met last Saturday when I began this Holy War against the War on Terrorism that George Bush is waging on the world told me that he has interviewed me four times this week already. He told me that he has never, ever interviewed anyone four times, let alone four times in one week. I was joking with the reporters that were here last week that they should have brought me flowers on our one-week anniversary.

The most fantabulistic (I needed a new word, none of the old ones fit) thing happened in Crawford today. There was a very insignificant counter-protest across the way. At first the sheriffs let them stand in the street, until we politely pointed out to the sheriffs that we had to stay in the ditch last week. So they made them move into the ditch. We are supposedly in Bush country, but the counter-protest was small and weak. They had signs that said, "Stay the Course." I appreciated that. I really believe they were telling me to stay the course. I will.

We also met a man whose son was KIA in Iraq in November of 2004. He still loves George Bush and thinks we are doing great things in Iraq. By the end of the day, we were drinking beer together and telling each other, "I love you." I am telling you, miracles are happening here in Crawford.

Anyway, back to the fantabulistic thing that happened today. We had a rally downtown in Crawford. Then the people caravanned up to Camp Casey. I was told to come down to the point of the triangle to greet them. While I was walking down to the point, I had a great view of Prairie Chapel Road. There was car, after car, after car!!! I started sobbing and I felt like collapsing. The cars kept on coming. It took almost a full hour for them to all get to Camp Casey. It was a miraculous sight to see. It was identical to *Field of Dreams*. People came from all over the country to be here. We are building a movement, and they are coming.

We don't have a full count of all the people who were there, but I would say hundreds. It was amazing and awesome. I felt the spirits of all of our needlessly killed loved ones in the presence of Camp Casey. I felt their strength and the wisdom of the ages with me in that wonderful place.

Two young ladies from San Diego drove all night to get to the rally, and they had to leave tonight to get back home. One of them said, "Wow, we can drive all the way from San Diego just to meet you, and he can't even come down to the end of his driveway to meet with you."

George Bush, you work for me. I pay your salary. Come out and talk to me. Anyway, I have a feeling you are about to be fired!!!

DAY NINE
"CASEY WOULD BE PROUD OF YOU"
Camp Casey, Sunday, August 14

The ninth day ended in the most awesome way. We were out at Camp Casey, and it was sprinkling a little bit, and it really looked like the rain was going to start pouring down any time. We looked over into the next cow pasture and there was a full rainbow. Rainbows are supposedly God's sign of hope. When Casey was killed on 04/04/04, I thought that all of my hope was killed, too. Being involved in the peaceful occupation of Crawford and meeting hundreds of people from all over the world have given me so much hope for the future.

We had a lovely interfaith prayer service this morning. It was truly beautiful, and we were all weeping while we were singing "Amazing Grace." But during the service, one of our neighbors fired off a shotgun. He said he was shooting at birds, but he is tired of us being there and he wants us to leave. I didn't get to talk to him, but I told the media that if he wanted us to leave so badly, why doesn't he tell his other neighbor, George, to talk to me. We are good neighbors and we are cooperating with everyone. By the way, in case I forgot to blog it last night, the sheriff has requested that I stay down in Crawford during the night, because he is afraid for my safety after he leaves. He said he would "sleep better" himself at night if I came into town to sleep. Judging from the shooting guns, I guess he was right.

George Bush took a two-hour bike ride on Saturday, and when he got back, he was asked how he could go for a two-hour bike ride when he doesn't have time to meet with me, and he said, "I have to go on with my life." *What!!!!?????* He has to get on with his life!!! I am so offended by that statement. Every person, war fan or not, who has had a child killed in this mistake of an occupation should be highly offended by that remark. Who does he think he is? I wish I could *ever* be able to get on with my life. Getting on with my life means a life without my dear, sweet boy. Getting on with my life means learning to live with a pain that is so intense that sometimes I feel like throwing up, or screaming until I pass out from sorrow. I wish a little bike ride could help me get on with my life.

I need to focus on the positive, though, and there is so much. I had so many amazing things happen today. I couldn't walk through Camp Casey or the Crawford Peace House today without hugging people and getting my picture taken. Now I know how Mickey Mouse feels at Disneyland. I had a soldier from Fort Hood come out today, and he brought me a small stone with a First Cavalry insignia painted on it and the pictures of three of his beautiful buddies who were murdered there by George's reckless policies. It was such an incredible moment for me when he said, "Keep on doing what you are doing. We are so proud of you. Casey would be so proud of you."

If George had as much courage in his entire body as Casey had in his little pinky, he would meet with me. Crawford, Texas, is beautiful prairie land, but I could think of dozens of other places I would rather be right now. However, if George or anybody else thinks I am leaving before my mission is "accomplished," they have another think coming. I will stay the course. I will finish the mission. I will take no prisoners.

By the way, we had about seven counter-protesters today and hundreds at Camp Casey. Don't let the mainstream media say differently.

DAY TEN

THIS IS GEORGE BUSH'S ACCOUNTABILITY MOMENT

Camp Casey, Monday, August 15

November 2, 2004, was not George Bush's accountability moment; today is. We are finished allowing him to get away with deceiving the American public and abusing his power. That's why I'm here. The mainstream media aren't holding him accountable. Neither is Congress. So I'm not leaving Crawford until he's held accountable. It's ironic, given the attacks leveled at me recently, how some in the media are so quick to scrutinize—and distort—the words and actions of a grieving mother but not the words and actions of the president of the United States.

But now it's time for him to level with me and with the American people. I think that's why there's been such an outpouring of support. This is giving the 61 percent of Americans who feel that the war is wrong something to do—something that allows their voices to be heard. It's a way for them to stand up and show that they *do* want our troops home, and that they know this war *is* a mistake, a mistake they want to see corrected. It's too late to bring back the people who are already dead, but there are tens of thousands of people still in harm's way.

There is too much at stake to worry about our own egos. When my son was killed, I had to face the fact that I was somehow also responsible for what happened. Every American who allows this to continue has, to some extent, blood on his or her hands. Some of us have a little bit, and some of us are soaked in it.

People have asked what it is I want to say to President Bush. Well, my message is a simple one. He said that my son— and the other children we've lost—died for a noble cause. I want to find out what that noble cause is. And I want to ask him, "If it's such a noble cause, have you asked your daughters to enlist? Have you encouraged them to go take the place of soldiers who are on their third tour of duty?" I also want him to stop using my son's name to justify the war. The idea that we have to "complete the mission" in Iraq to honor Casey's sacrifice is, to me, a sacrilege to my son's name. Besides, does the president any longer even know what "the mission" really is over there?

Casey knew that the war was wrong from the beginning. But he felt it was his duty to go, that his buddies were going, and that he had no choice. The people who send our young, honorable, brave soldiers to die in this war have no skin in the game. They don't have any loved ones in harm's way. As for people like O'Reilly and Hannity and Michelle Malkin and Rush Limbaugh and all the others who are attacking me and parroting the administration line that we must complete the mission there—they don't have one thing at stake. They don't suffer through sleepless nights worrying about their loved ones.

Before this all started, I used to think that one person couldn't make a difference, but now I see that one person who has the backing and support of millions of people can make a huge difference.

That's why I'm going to be out here until one of three things happens: It's August 31 and the president's vacation ends and he leaves Crawford, they take me away in a squad car, or the president finally agrees to speak with me.

If he does, he'd better be prepared for me to hold his feet to the fire. If he starts talking about freedom and democracy—or about how the war in Iraq is protecting America—I'm not going to let him get away with it.

Like I said, this is George Bush's accountability moment. All we're asking is that he sacrifice an hour out of his five-week vacation to talk to us. We are mad as hell, and we're not taking it anymore.

Thank you all.

DAY TEN

LEAVE MY FAMILY ALONE

Camp Casey, Monday, August 15 (Blog Entry #2)

I apparently am the sacrificial lamb of the peace movement. I don't care about myself. Putting myself in the forefront and daring to challenge the president on his lies left me open to the attacks, which are, of course, half-truths and distortions.

But when they start sliming my home life and my family, that's where I draw the line. Yes, my husband has filed for divorce, and yes, he filed before I left for the Veterans for Peace convention and this trip to Crawford, and yes, *it is between my husband and me.*

Having Casey murdered in Iraq by George Bush's reckless policies has been hard enough on my family, but my setting off on my holy war to bring the troops home, my constant absences, and all of the media attention have put additional stresses on my family.

I chose my path after Casey died. The rest of the family have chosen theirs. We all still love each other and support each other in anything that we do. We didn't want Casey to join the Army, but once he made that decision, we supported him and even encouraged him through boot camp.

We are a normal American family who have had good times, bad times, and terrible times. We hope the good times will come back. We hope that we will be able to laugh with abandon together like we used to one day. We hope that the troops come home and no other families have to go through what we are going through.

It isn't about politics for us. No one asked Casey what political affiliation he was before they sent him off to die in Iraq, and no one asked us who we voted for in 2000 before we were handed a folded flag from Casey's flag-draped coffin.

I am not perfect, and I never even claimed to be perfect. My family isn't perfect, but we are pretty special, especially the children. We all miss Casey so much, and it is George Bush and his neocon cabal who are at fault. The people who are dragging my family through the mud need to grow up and look at themselves. The Christ said, "He who is without sin, cast the first stone."

If everyone followed Jesus' advice, the world would be a much better place.

DAY ELEVEN

PUTTING OUT FIRES

Camp Casey, Tuesday, August 16

The right-wingers are really having a field day with me. It hurts me really badly, but I am willing to put up with the crap if it ends the war a minute sooner than it would have. I would like to address some specific concerns that have been raised against me.

The first one is about my divorce. I addressed this on my blog last night. My divorce was in the works way before I came out to Crawford. My husband filed the papers before this all started. It just was recorded last Friday. My husband didn't know that it would become public record and public knowledge. He had told his lawyer not to serve me with the paperwork or even bother me while I was at Camp Casey. He was trying to do the right thing. He didn't want me to find out. Enough about that.

Another "big deal" today was the lie that I had said that Casey died for Israel. I never said that, I never wrote that. I had supposedly said it in a letter that I wrote to Ted Koppel's producer in March. I wrote the letter because I was upset at the way Ted treated me when I appeared at a *Nightline* town hall meeting in January right after the inauguration. I felt that Ted had totally disrespected me. I wrote the letter to Ted Bettag and cc'd the person who gave me Ted's address. I believe he changed the e-mail and sent it out to capitalize on my newfound notoriety by promoting his own agenda. Enough about that.

I didn't blog about the cross incident last night. I was at the Peace House when there was a big commotion and people started saying that someone had run over our Arlington Crawford display. I know this is old news, because I have seen great posts about it today. This is how I feel. The right-wingers are e-mailing me and spewing filth about me on the radio and on the television saying that I am dishonoring my son's memory. This man who ran over the crosses thinks he is a better American than we are. He thinks he is more patriotic than we are. Does he really believe that he is honoring the memories of the fallen and his country by running down 500 crosses and about 60 American flags? The Iraq Veterans Against the War who were here were also very offended. Those crosses represented their buddies who didn't make it home. And they are so aware of the fact that one of those crosses could have their name on it.

Yesterday, we had a counter-protestor who played his guitar across the way from us and sang (very terribly!!!) a song that loosely went like this:

Aiding and abetting the enemy.
How many ghosts did you make today?
Google me this, Google me that,
How many ghosts did you make today?

I find it so ironic that he was singing it to me, and not to George Bush. We named the song "The Ballad of George Bush." He came back out today, but blessed be to God, he didn't bring his guitar, and he didn't sing.

We are moving to a place that doesn't have much shade, and I put out an appeal for tarps and a soldier from Fort Hood brought some to us that he "borrowed" from Fort Hood for us to use. I have had a lot of soldiers from Fort Hood come out and tell me to keep it up and that I am doing a good thing. We are doing this to honor Casey and the other fallen heroes, in their memory. But we are doing it *for* the people of Iraq and the other soldiers who are in harm's way right now. Right after we heard about the crosses last night, a Camp Casey volunteer found out that a pen pal she had in Iraq was KIA on August 12. This has to stop, now. We will stop it.

The president says he feels compassion for me, but the best way to show that compassion is by meeting with me and the other mothers and families who are here. Our sons made the ultimate sacrifice and we want answers. All we're asking is that he sacrifice an hour out of his five-week vacation to talk to us, before the next mother loses her son in Iraq.

DAY ELEVEN

MISSES AND MIRACLES

Camp Casey, Tuesday, August 16 (Blog Entry #2)

We still have so many great things happening at Camp Casey. In spite of all the smears and lies, people are still coming.

The most amazing thing today was learning that Camp Caseys are opening and spreading all over the country. They have been set up in Boston, Portland, Seattle, and elsewhere. If you can't make it to Camp Casey, set up your own version. Camp Caseys are amazing places full of love and hope. I am so gratified that the movement is spreading.

There is a meeting tomorrow of the county commissioners to vote on closing Prairie Chapel Road and then evicting us. We were all worried about that and planning on being arrested when we got the best news yet. The property owner who owns property near Bush's ranch and right across the street from Bush's church will let us move Camp Casey there!! He has property on both sides of the road—a full acre for us to camp! We are so excited!!! We can fit more people, and we will be closer to the ranch. Miracles, miracles.

Mike Rogers from Tokyo showed up today, and a dear woman from Australia who was a human shield in Iraq and knows that the Iraqi people are not jumping for joy for the policies of Bush that destroyed their country.

This is an extremely short post today. I am exhausted.

DAY TWELVE

VIGILS

Camp Casey, Wednesday, August 17

Our candlelight vigil at Camp Casey was beautiful tonight. There were hundreds of people here, and we are hearing that thousands of people were involved in vigils around the country. We at Camp Casey are so amazed and gratified that there were almost 1700 vigils around the country.

CNN followed me around for the morning to do "A Day in the Life of Cindy Sheehan." I kept asking them if they were falling asleep from boredom yet. I was on Anderson Cooper, and it was pretty good. Anderson didn't ask me about the Israel thing, because he had checked with *Nightline*. But he followed with a talk-show hate-monger host, Darrell Ankarlo, whom I have had problems with in the past. He said that I have said that I believe all of the troops are murderers, and I have never said that either. Darrell Ankarlo wanted me to be on his show, but I don't think so.

Another thing is that the Israel thing has not died. I did not say that my son died for Israel. I have never said it, I don't think it, and I don't believe it. It is just another lie, smear tactic from the right. It needs to die right now. It's not the truth. I stand by everything that I have said. But I will not stand by things that I haven't said. I am not anti-Semitic. I am just anti-killing. George Bush is responsible for killing so many people, but nobody scrutinizes anything he says, especially leading up to the war. Since there is nothing to smear me about with the truth, they have to tell lies. A former friend who is anti-Israel and wants to use the spotlight on me to push his anti-Semitism is telling everyone who is listening that I believe that Casey died for Israel and has gone so far as to apparently doctor an e-mail from me. People have to know that he doesn't speak for me. ABC *Nightline* can't confirm that his e-mail is real, and therefore any reporting on it is irresponsible. That is not my issue. That is not my message, and anyone who knows me knows it doesn't sound like me.

I'm focused on my mission in Crawford: to meet with the president and demand answers. That's it. I have spent enough time on that. Enough is enough.

So tonight was a great night, with the vigil capping it off. There are so many good things happening around the country. I love the people of America, especially after seeing the most amazing stories from the vigils across the country.

Day Thirteen

It's Not About Me,
It's About the War

Camp Casey, Thursday, August 18

Even after my repeated attempts to keep the focus of my protest on the war, the Drudge Report and others continue to try to make the issue about me. But I am not the issue. The issue is a disastrous war that's killing our sons and daughters and making our country less secure. They attack me because they can no longer defend this war.

I've come to Crawford to bring to the president's doorstep the harsh realities of a war he's been trying so hard to avoid. But no matter what they say or how many shotguns they fire or how many crosses they destroy, they're not going to stop me from speaking out about a war that needlessly killed my son.

Day Thirteen

Leaving Camp Casey

Thursday, August 18 (Blog Entry #2)

Today started out okay. I did my usual stint with Marc and Mark on the *Morning Sedition* on Air America Radio. I always love talking to them because they are so funny and smart. We have a 7:10 a.m. time. *Nightline* was also following me to do a

"Day in the Life of Cindy Sheehan" piece, so they got there nice and early to mic me up. I gave two interviews early this morning where I said that the Camp Casey peace movement has taken on a life of its own. With all of the vigils last night and the Camp Caseys springing up all over the country, nothing can stop it, not even me. I said that if I had to leave today, the movement would continue to prosper and grow.

The only thing that Matt Drudge could dig up on me today was a speech I had given at a "College-Not-Combat" rally at San Francisco State where I said some cuss words. This posting of his may be the first true thing he has ever said about me. I wonder, though, if any of the words I used shocked him. I wonder if he has ever used those words himself. I wonder if he has ever had a child killed by senseless violence in a war that is such a waste.

Some Gold Star moms from Oregon joined me today and another from California. Another mom whose son was killed this past February arrived last night. Then we had a Gold Star dad whose son had died this past June 15 show up at Camp Casey today with his family. Ruben said he just came to give me a hug. He said until today he had felt so lonely. Every time I meet a Gold Star parent whose child died after Casey, I feel so bad. I have been struggling for months to call attention to this mistake of a war to end it sooner. Every new death is like a stab in my heart.

Even what Rush Limbaugh said about me yesterday, although very idiotic, wasn't really bothering me that much because it is so ridiculous. He said that I am not real, my son is not real, and Camp Casey is not real!!!???? He said my entire story is based on "forged documents." I wonder just exactly what he meant. Did he mean that Casey's KIA report is forged? Did we bury an empty coffin on April 13, 2004? Am I just a really good actress playing a grieving mom? Does he realize how much I wish that all this were true? He is a clanging gong!

How can anyone say anything so monstrous and so obviously false, and how can anyone believe him?

So, although a scorching day in Crawford, things were going pretty well. We were planning our move and what turned out to be a successful mothers' march up to the ranch to deliver some letters to Laura Bush. Then my sister received the phone call from a hospital in California: our mother had a stroke. We were on a plane from Waco heading to Dallas within two hours. The cameras beat us to the airport in Waco and filmed me getting my ticket, waiting to go through security, and actually going through security. As I sit writing this on the plane from Dallas to Los Angeles, I am sure there will be a mob of cameras waiting to greet me in L.A. (Apparently whether I am walking to the outhouse at Camp Casey or through a small airport in Texas, it is fascinating stuff.) The camera guys all wished us well and sent their best wishes to our mom, though. The camera and sound guys and I have been spending lots of time together lately.

I hated leaving Camp Casey, but this is a family emergency and the doctor couldn't really tell us about the status of our mother by phone. I couldn't bear to be worrying about her from so far away. We are carrying Camp Casey with us in our hearts, though, and Camp Casey will be moved to its new location and thriving when I get back.

In the first paragraph, I told you that the Camp Casey movement will continue to grow and thrive even if I am not there. Dozens of people work so hard to keep it going. Now we shall see. I am sure it will be fantabulistic.

"PEACE MOM" LEAVES CAMP, HER MOTHER ILL

by Angela K. Brown
The Associated Press

Thursday, August 18, Crawford, Texas

Crawford, Texas—The grieving mother who started an anti-war demonstration near President Bush's ranch nearly two weeks ago said Thursday she was leaving because her mother had a stroke.

Cindy Sheehan told reporters she had just received the phone call and would rush to her 74-year-old mother's side. Her mother lives in the Los Angeles area.

"I'll be back as soon as possible if it's possible," Sheehan said. After hugging some of her supporters, she got in a van and left.

Sheehan, of Vacaville, Calif., said the makeshift campsite off the road leading to Bush's ranch would continue. The camp has grown to more than 100 people, including many relatives of soldiers killed in Iraq.

Sheehan had vowed to remain until Bush met with her or until his month-long vacation was over.

"I WANT TO GET BACK AS SOON AS POSSIBLE"

Interview on *Democracy Now!*

Broadcast Friday, August 19

AMY GOODMAN: Last night, when we came into Dallas/Fort Worth Airport, we actually crossed paths with Cindy. She was planning to stay here during the entire time that President Bush is vacationing, but yesterday afternoon she learned in a telephone call that her mother had suffered a stroke in Los Angeles, California, and so she and her sister Dede dropped everything here, and they raced to Waco to the airport, flew to the Dallas/Fort Worth Airport, where we were just coming in from New York, the *Democracy Now!* crew. We met her at her gate and sat down and had a conversation with Cindy to find out how she's doing, but also to find out what her plans are.

This is Cindy Sheehan, the woman who began it all here just a few weeks ago when she left a Veterans for Peace annual meeting in Dallas and headed to President Bush's ranch, asking if he would simply have a meeting with her. I asked her yesterday at the airport how her mother was.

CINDY SHEEHAN: It's too early to tell. She was still in the emergency room when we left, so we didn't get any messages from my brother, who is there with her right now. So, hopefully, the status hasn't changed since we last talked to him.

AMY GOODMAN: What do you think it means for you to leave Crawford, for you to leave the ranch where President Bush is vacationing?

CINDY SHEEHAN: Well, it's kind of ironic, because this morning I gave two interviews, one to Air America and one to

Nightline early this morning. And I said, "You know what, this Camp Casey movement is bigger than me. It's growing. It's bigger than any of us. And even if I had to leave today, it would keep on going. And if we leave August 31 without the president speaking to us, it's going to keep on." It's growing. It's organic. It's here, and nothing is going to stop it. And just because I'm gone—things will just carry on as normal. I want to get back as soon as possible, because I did say I would stay there until President Bush spoke with me or until he left on August 31. I hope if he comes out and speaks to the other moms that they give him hell, though.

AMY GOODMAN: How many other moms are there of people who are in Iraq or who have died in Iraq?

CINDY SHEEHAN: We have about six Gold Star moms, and maybe about the same number, or a little more, of women who have children over there right now.

AMY GOODMAN: Your reaction to the more than 1500 vigils that were held around the country on Wednesday night?

CINDY SHEEHAN: It, to me, is just absolutely amazing and so gratifying that something I did—like, I was just a spark that just lit this fire, and it's blazing, and it's out of control now. Like I said, we don't need the spark anymore, and I am just— I'm just so grateful that the universe chose me to be the spark, but also that America has responded. I'm grateful and amazed, but I'm not surprised, because I have seen this coming.

AMY GOODMAN: If you get this meeting with President Bush, what will you say to him?

CINDY SHEEHAN: I want to ask him what was the noble cause that Casey and the others have died for, because he keeps on saying that they died for a noble cause, and I don't think a war of aggression against a nation that was no threat to the United States of America is a noble cause. And I'm not going to let him tell me about keeping America safe for freedom and democracy, because he told us before he invaded that it was about weapons of mass destruction and Saddam Hussein with some kind of a link to al Qaeda. And that's been proven wrong, and it's been proven wrong consistently, and the Downing Street Memo proves that as early as July of 2002, they knew that that was wrong and they had to fabricate the intelligence to fit their policy of invading Iraq. And that means that my son's murder was premeditated.

AMY GOODMAN: Where did your son die?

CINDY SHEEHAN: He died in Sadr City, Baghdad, in an ambush on April 4, 2004.

AMY GOODMAN: What was his understanding of why he was going there?

CINDY SHEEHAN: He thought it was probably for oil, and he didn't want to go. He didn't agree that the president was using his troops wisely. And I begged him not to go, and he said, "Mom, I have to go. My buddies are going." And if I had known that, you know, if I had known what was going to happen to him, I think I probably would have tried to force him into Canada or something, but, you know, he was an adult, and he thought it was his duty, and so I was as supportive as I could be. He was only there for five days, though, before he was killed.

AMY GOODMAN: There is a major right-wing attack on you led by Bill O'Reilly, the Drudge Report. They call you a traitor. Your response?

CINDY SHEEHAN: I believe that it is my right and responsibility as an American to question our government when our government is wrong. I'm not one of the immature patriots who say my country, right or wrong, because my country is wrong now, and my country—the policies of my country—are responsible for killing tens of thousands of innocent people, and I won't stand by and let that happen anymore. And I believe that anybody who tries to tell me that I don't have the right to say what I'm saying, they're unpatriotic, they're un-American, and their attacks are not going to stop me.

AMY GOODMAN: Are you going to follow President Bush back to the White House? Are you going to follow him from now on?

CINDY SHEEHAN: We're going to do a bus tour from Crawford to D.C. on the thirty-first, and it's going to—we're going to take three buses through different parts of the country, going through different cities, picking up different people, and we're going to converge together on D.C. on September 24 for the big United for Peace and Justice rally. And I won't be able to be on those buses, because I have commitments. My entire month of September is committed. And it was even before I decided to do this, so I'm going to be meeting up with everybody on September 24 in D.C. And then we'll see where we're going to go from there.

AMY GOODMAN: Do you plan on taking up the same vigil in Lafayette Park outside the White House?

CINDY SHEEHAN: There's a group of us planning on doing that. I won't, of course, be able to be there twenty-four hours a day forever, but it's going to be like a rotating vigil. And then when he goes back to Crawford, we'll go back to Crawford.

AMY GOODMAN: That is Cindy Sheehan. She was speaking to us at Dallas/Fort Worth Airport, as she caught the next plane to Los Angeles to see her ailing mother. Her mother had a stroke yesterday. She is 74 years old. Cindy Sheehan, co-founder of Gold Star Families for Peace, also founder of Camp Casey, named for her son, Casey Sheehan, who died April 4, 2004, in Iraq in Sadr City.

DAY FOURTEEN

MY MOM

Los Angeles, Friday, August 19

I spent a majority of the day in the hospital with my mom. She seems to be getting stronger by the minute thanks to all the prayers and well wishes from the world. I am so grateful for all of the love and support we are getting right now.

My mom is still in ICU and I don't know if she will ever be able to come home, but I know she knows we are there, and we even made her laugh a couple of times today, even though she can't speak.

I hear things are going great at Camp Casey and more Gold Star Families for Peace members are arriving every day. They want to say, "We want to speak to the president, too. He killed our sons, brothers, and dads, too. We are tired of being disrespected and lied to. We deserve the truth and we deserve respect."

Something George Bush *et al.* refuse to acknowledge is that *he works for us.* He is our employee. Did we forget that too, as a nation? I think we did, but I think we are waking up and remembering that we have the power. *We* are the government. We have everything it takes to make change possible. I used to have doubts about 2006 and the progressives' chances of taking over at least one branch of our government, but now I think it is so possible. We will kick some fat booty in 2006, and we will change America for the better. *We can do it!!!*

What started in Crawford on August 6 is an amazing testament to the American people. I knew we had it in us. I knew we could do it. I had faith in us, and my faith was rewarded.

Thank you all for your prayers, phone calls, and e-mails. With the love of my family, friends, Camp Casey, and you all, I will be back soon.

DAY FIFTEEN

THE CAMP CASEY MOVEMENT
WILL NOT DIE

Los Angeles, Saturday, August 20

The media are wrong. The people who have come out to Camp Casey to help coordinate the press and events with me are not putting words in my mouth. They are taking words out of my mouth. I have been known for some time as a person who speaks the truth and speaks it strongly. I have always called a liar a liar and a hypocrite a hypocrite. Now I am urged to use softer language to appeal to a wider audience. Why do my friends at Camp Casey think they are there? Why did such a big movement occur from such a small action on August 6, 2005?

I haven't had much time to analyze the Camp Casey phenomenon. I just read that I gave 250 interviews in less than a week's time. I believe it. I would go to bed with a raw throat every night. I got pretty tired of answering some questions, like: "What do you want to say to the president?" and "Do you really think he will meet with you?" However, since my mom has been sick, I have had a chance to step back and ponder the floodgates that I opened in Crawford, Texas.

I just read an article posted today on LewRockwell.com by artist Robert Shetterly, who painted my portrait. The article reminded me of something I said at the Veterans for Peace convention the night before I set out for Bush's ranch in my probably futile quest for the truth. This is what I said: "I got an e-mail the other day and it said, 'Cindy if you didn't use so much profanity ... there are people on the fence that get offended." And you know what I said? "You know what? If you fall on the side that is pro-George and pro-war, you get your ass over to Iraq, and take the place of somebody who wants to come home. And if you fall on the side that is against this war and against George Bush, stand up and speak out."

This is what the Camp Casey miracle is all about: American citizens who oppose the war but never had a conduit for their disgust and dismay are dropping everything and traveling to Crawford to stand in solidarity with us who have made a commitment to sit outside of George's ranch for the duration of the miserable Texas August. If they can't come to Texas, they are attending vigils, writing letters to their elected officials and to their local newspapers; they are setting up Camp Casey branches in their hometowns; they are sending flowers, cards, letters, gifts, and donations here to us at Camp Casey. We are so grateful for all of the support, but I think pro-peace Americans are grateful for something to do, finally.

One thing I haven't noticed or become aware of, though, is an increased number of pro-war, pro-Bush people on the other side of the fence enlisting to go and fight George Bush's war for imperialism and insatiable greed. The pro-peace side has gotten off their apathetic butts to be warriors for peace and justice. Where are the pro-war people? Every day at Camp Casey we have a couple of anti-peace people on the other side of the road holding up signs that remind me that "Freedom Isn't Free," but I don't see them putting their money where their mouths are. I don't think they are willing to pay even a small down payment for freedom by sacrificing their own blood or the flesh of their children. I still challenge them to go to Iraq and let another soldier come home—perhaps a soldier who is on his or her third tour of duty, or one who has been stop-lossed after serving his or her country nobly and selflessly, only to be held hostage in Iraq by power-mad hypocrites who have a long history of avoiding putting their own skin in the game.

Contrary to what the mainstream media thinks, I did not just fall off a pumpkin truck in Crawford, Texas, on that scorchingly hot day two weeks ago. I have been writing, speaking, testifying in front of congressional committees, lobbying Congress, and doing interviews for over a year now. I have been pretty well known in the progressive, peace community, and I had many, many supporters before I even left California. The people who supported me did so because they know that I uncompromisingly tell the truth about this war. I have stood up and said, "My son died for *nothing*, and George Bush and his evil cabal and their reckless policies killed him. My son was sent to fight in a war that had no basis in reality and was killed for it." I have never said "pretty please" or "thank you." I have never said anything wishy-washy the way that George Bush uses patriotic rhetoric. I say my son died for *lies*. George Bush *lied* to us, and he knew he was *lying*. The Downing Street Memo, dated July 23, 2002, proves that he knew that Saddam didn't have WMDs or any ties to al Qaeda. George made us afraid of ghosts that weren't there. Now he is using patriotic rhetoric to keep the U.S. military presence in Iraq, patriotic rhetoric that is based on greed and nothing else.

Now I am being vilified and dragged through the mud by the righties and so-called "fair and balanced" mainstream media who are afraid of the truth and can't face someone who tells it by telling any truth of their own. Now they have to twist, distort, lie, and scrutinize anything I have ever said when they never scrutinize anything that George Bush said or is saying. Instead of asking George or Scotty McClellan if he will meet with me, why aren't they asking the questions they should have been asking all along: "Why are our young people fighting, dying, and killing in Iraq? What is this noble cause you are sending our young people to Iraq for? What do you hope to accomplish there? Why did you tell us there were WMDs and ties to al Qaeda when you knew there weren't? Why did you lie to us? Why did you lie to the American people? Why did you lie to the world? Why are our nation's children still in harm's way and dying every day when we all know you lied? Why do you continually say we have to 'complete the mission' when you know damn well you have no idea what that mission is and you change it at will like you change your cowboy shirts?"

Camp Casey has grown and prospered and survived all attacks and challenges because America is sick and tired of liars and hypocrites, and we want the answers to the tough questions that I was the first to dare ask. *This* is George Bush's accountability moment, and he is failing miserably. George Bush and his advisers seriously "misunderestimated" me when they thought they could intimidate me into leaving before I had the answers or before the end of August. I can take anything they throw at me or Camp Casey. If it shortens the war by a minute or saves one life, it is worth it. I think they seriously "misunderestimated" all mothers. I wonder if any of them had authentic mother-child relationships and if they are surprised that there are so many mothers in this country who are bearlike when it comes to wanting the truth and who want to make meaning of their children's needless and seemingly meaningless deaths.

The Camp Casey movement will not die until we have a genuine accounting of the truth and until our troops are brought home. Get used to it, George. We are not going away.

DAY SEVENTEEN

GO HOME AND TAKE CARE OF YOUR KIDS

Los Angeles, Monday, August 22

I have received dozens of e-mails with this heading: Go Home and Take Care of Your Kids. I think of all the name-calling and unnecessary and untrue trashing of my character, this one offends me the most. What do the people who send me this message mean?

First of all, it offends me because it is so blatantly sexist. Would anyone think of e-mailing George Bush when he is out and about (now he is going on a vacation away from his vacation to make speeches in Idaho and Utah defending his killing policies), telling him to go and take care of his kids? Does anyone write to *any* man and tell him to go home and take care of his kids? I have news for all of these people: my children are adults, and their dad is home to take care of them if they need any taking care of.

The second reason this command from the self-righteous right offends me is that I believe that what I am doing is for my children, and the world's children. I think that the strategy of eternal, baseless war for corporate profit and greed is bad for all of our children, born and unborn. We heard a few weeks ago that Rummy said that we would be in Iraq for at least a dozen more years, and we recently heard over the weekend that the military is planning for four more years of this occupation, at least. If Rummy is correct, then Soccer Safety Mom Susie's kindergartener will be fighting and dying in the harsh sands of the Middle East, and if the military is correct, then NASCAR Dad Nick's middle-schooler should start boot camp now. I hate to be the one to break it to America, but constant war is not a positive family value, and this administration's policies are not making us more secure.

We as mothers need to stop buying into the load of misogynistic crap that our children need our constant presence in their lives so they can thrive and grow. What we need as families are strong support systems that allow each family member to grow and achieve his or her full potential as a human being. What we as moms need to stop doing is giving our children to the military-industrial war complex to be used as human cluster bombs: to kill innocent civilians and to perhaps die enriching and feeding the gluttonous war machine.

It is up to us moms to make sure our children are whole and safe. We can start doing this by always opposing the wars that bury our kids before us. So this is what I am saying to the people who want me to go home and take care of my kids: I *am* taking care of my kids, and yours, too.

DAY EIGHTEEN

MY RESPONSE TO GEORGE AS HE SPEAKS FROM HIS VACATION AWAY FROM HIS VACATION

Los Angeles, Tuesday, August 23

(Paragraphs in italics are from an Associated Press story.)

President Bush charged Tuesday that antiwar protesters like Cindy Sheehan who want troops brought home immediately do not represent the views of most U.S. military families and are "advocating a policy that would weaken the United States."

Bringing our troops home from the quagmire that he has gotten us into will weaken the United States? George, even if you pretend you didn't know that Saddam did not have weapons of mass destruction and Iraq was not a threat to the USA before you invaded, Americans know differently. We have read the reports and the Downing Street Memos. We know you had to "fit the intelligence around the policy" of invading Iraq. I want to know what your real reasons were.

In brief remarks outside the resort where he is vacationing, Bush gave no indication that he would change his mind and meet with Sheehan after he returns to his Texas ranch Wednesday evening. Sheehan lost a son in Iraq and has emerged as a harsh critic of the war.

I will be back in Crawford, George, even closer to you now in Camp Casey II. Why don't you channel some courage from my son and come down and face me. Face the truth. Your house of cards, built on smoke and mirrors, is crumbling, and you know it.

Sheehan has been maintaining a vigil outside Bush's ranch, a demonstration that has been joined by more and more other anti-war protesters.

Because I am not the only one in America who wants the answers—America wants the answers.

Bush said that two high-ranking members of his staff already met with her earlier this month and that he met with her last year.

I didn't go to Crawford to meet with Steven "yellow-cake uranium liar" Hadley or the other "high-ranking" official they sent out. I went to meet with George. Does he get that yet? I did meet with him ten weeks after his insane and arrogant Iraq war policies killed Casey and nine weeks after I buried my oldest child. George, things are different between you and me now.

"I've met with a lot of families," Bush said. "She doesn't represent the view of a lot of families I have met with."

I never said I did. I want one answer: What is the "noble cause" my son died for. There are also dozens, if not hundreds, of families from all over the country who want to know the same thing.

On Iraq, Bush said that a democratic constitution "is going to be an important change in the broader Middle East." Reaching an accord on a constitution after years of dictatorship is not easy, Bush said.

A democratic constitution? Is anyone else insulted that he thinks we are stupid and think that the constitution they will form in Iraq will be democratic and ensure equal rights to all citizens? Does anyone else know what "democratic" means? It simply means majority rule. Not some high-minded, free-floating, pie-in-the-sky ideal. It means 50 percent plus 1. Up to 62 percent of Americans think our troops should be coming home soon. That is a majority, so why don't we force our employee, the president, to do what we want him to do?

He spoke after the head of the committee drafting Iraq's constitution said Tuesday that three days are not enough to win over the minority Sunni Arabs, and the document they rejected may ultimately have to be approved by parliament as is and submitted to the people in a referendum.

Another sham election where the country is shut down for the day and no one knows what the heck they are voting for?

"The Iraqi people are working hard to reach a consensus on their constitution," Bush said, speaking outside the Tamarack Resort, in the mountains one hundred miles north of Boise. "It's an amazing process to work. First of all, the fact that they're even writing a constitution is vastly different from living under the iron hand of a dictator."

As hard as George is working riding bikes and taking naps? If he cares so much about an Iraqi constitution, why doesn't he take some time from his busy vacation activities and read the U.S. Constitution. He may find out that he started an unconstitutional war in Iraq. He may lose some sleep over it. (What am I saying?)

"The Sunnis have got to make a choice," Bush said. "Do they want to live in a society that's free? Or do they want to live in violence?"

Too bad George didn't give them that option before he invaded and occupied their country, resulting in the deaths of tens of thousands of innocent people. I bet they would choose to live in a peaceful country, free of foreign occupiers.

He said he thought that most mothers, regardless of their religion, would prefer to live in peace rather than violence.

Amen to that George. You got one thing right. Thanks to you and your lies, the people of Iraq are suffering from a tragic and unnecessary war, and my son was violently killed and ripped out of the heart of our family.

He said Rice had assured him that the rights of women were being protected. "Democracy is unfolding," the president said. "We just cannot tolerate the status quo."

Then bring our troops home. The status quo in Iraq is awful. Besides the Iraqi people's suffering from lack of adequate infrastructure, clean water, and medical attention, our troops still don't have armored Humvees or the proper body armor. I got a letter from a soldier over in Iraq who says that he feels like an innocent man in prison. All of the soldiers and Marines who contact me say that they were lied to about the "mission." They were told that they would be rebuilding the country, and all they are doing is trying to survive so their moms won't go through what I am going through.

I think the Camp Casey movement is taking a hold and growing because America is sick of the status quo. We are sick of needless death and suffering on both sides. We are sick of paying for a war with our taxes and with our lifeblood that is not making our country more secure. George, your employers cannot tolerate the status quo, either.

On Sheehan, the grieving mother who has camped near his ranch since August 6, the president said he strongly supports her right to protest. "She expressed her opinion. I disagree with it," Bush said. "I think immediate withdrawal from Iraq would be a mistake," he said. "I think those who advocate immediate withdrawal from not only Iraq but the Middle East are advocating a policy that would weaken the United States."

This is the biggest smokescreen from him yet. Whether to bring the troops home now was not one of the questions I went to Crawford to ask the president. I asked him what Noble Cause did Casey die for? I am still waiting for one of the press corps to ask him that. I am still waiting for that answer. First, we were told WMDs: false. Then we were told Saddam = Osama: false. Then we were told Saddam was a bad man to his own people and we had to get rid of him: he's gone. Then we were told the Iraqi people had to have elections: they did. Now we are spreading "freedom and democracy," but we are building fourteen permanent bases, some the size of Sacramento, California. To me that indicates that we are spreading the cancer of imperialism and usurping *their* natural resources.

Bush has scheduled more than two hours to meet with family members of slain soldiers Wednesday at the Mountain Home Air Force Base near Boise.

I am just asking for an hour from his vacation, and he just has to come down the road, not travel to Idaho. I wonder if any of the handpicked family members will ask what noble cause their child died for. I hope so.

Bush said he planned to go on a hike and have dinner later Tuesday with Kempthorne and the Idaho congressional delegation. Bush said he also planned to spend "quality time" with first lady Laura Bush, who is traveling with him.

I would give everything I own, will own, or have owned to have one more glimpse of my son. Dare I even say, one last hug or phone call? How dare he go on vacation and live a normal life when he has ruined mine by his lies? How dare he take five weeks off when he is waging a devastating and needless war?

Bush, who is seeking to quell growing criticism at home over the Iraq war, told the Veterans of Foreign Wars national convention in Salt Lake City on Monday that "a policy of retreat and isolation will not bring us safety."

His policies of preemptive wars of aggression for power and greed don't bring America safety, either.

Bush made a rare reference to the U.S. military death toll—more than 2,000 killed in the Afghanistan and Iraq wars. "We owe them something. We will finish the task that they gave their lives for . . . by staying on the offensive against the terrorists, and building strong allies in Afghanistan and Iraq that will help us win and fight—fight and win the war on terror," he told the Veterans of Foreign Wars convention.

How does he honor the soldiers by killing more of their buddies? People say Casey is ashamed of me and I dishonor his memory! I knew my son better than anyone on earth, and I know he is appalled by the continued carnage in his name. George, you can't win the war on terror by killing more of our soldiers and innocent Iraqi people. You are breeding more terror. And judging from the fact that you are now tied with the worst president in U.S. history (Nixon) in your abysmal poll numbers, the people of our country realize this, too, and want you stopped.

DAY EIGHTEEN
COMING BACK TO CRAWFORD
Los Angeles, Tuesday, August 23 (Blog Entry #2)

I'm coming back to Crawford for my son. As long as the president, who sent him to die in a senseless war, is in Crawford, that is where I belong. I came here two-and-a-half weeks ago for one reason—to try to see the president and get an answer to a very simple question: What is the noble cause that he says my son died for?

The answer to that question will not bring my son back. But it may stop more meaningless deaths. Because every death is now a meaningless one. And the vast majority of our country knows this. So why do more young men and women have to die? And why do more parents have to lose their children and live the rest of their lives with this unbearable grief?

The presidency is not bigger than the people's will.

And when the people speak out, it's the president's responsibility to listen. He is there to serve us, not the other way around.

This isn't about politics. It's about what is good for America and what's best for our security and how far this president has taken us away from both.

I'm coming back to Crawford because—now and forever—this is my duty for my son, for my other children, for other parents, and for my country.

DAY NINETEEN

"GOOD JOB, MOM"

Camp Casey, Wednesday, August 24

I got up really early today to head back to Camp Casey. On the way, I had some amazing conversations with people. In one of those conversations, I was talking to Tyler, who was sitting next to me on one of the planes. We were not talking about me and what I have been doing. Randomly, he told me he had just been in Texas about an hour north of Crawford. I said, "Wow, that's where I am going and that's where I have been all month." He said, "I know. I own a television." I thought that was pretty cute.

I got to Camp Casey, and I arrived with a mom whose son, John, was killed on January 26, 2005, and John's wife and his baby, who never met his dad. We arrived in Waco at about 4:30 to the local press. The White House press corps was still with the president.

When I arrived at Camp Casey II this afternoon, I was amazed at what has changed since I left. Now we have a huge tent to get out of the sun, caterers, an orientation tent, a medic tent (with medics), a chapel, etcetera.

The most emotional thing for me though was walking through the main tent and seeing the huge painting on canvas of Casey. Many things hit me all at once—that this huge movement began because of Casey's sacrifice; that thousands, if not millions, of people know about Casey and how he lived his life and the wrongful way in which he was killed—but the thing that hit me the hardest was how much I miss him. I miss him more every day. It seems the void in my life grows as time goes on, and I realize I am never going to see him again or hear his voice. In addition to all this, the portrait is so beautiful and moving and it captures Casey's spirit so well. I sobbed and sobbed. I was surrounded by photographers. I looked around until I finally found a friendly face, and then the news people crushed in on me, and I couldn't breathe. I didn't mean to have such a dramatic re-entry to Camp Casey, but the huge portrait of Casey really surprised me.

I can take all of the right-wing attacks on me. I have been lied about and to before. Their attacks just show how much I am getting to them and how little truth they have to tell. What really hurts me the most is when people say that I am dishonoring Casey by my protest in Crawford. By wanting our troops to come home alive and well, that I am somehow not supporting them.

So, after Joan Baez gave us a great concert tonight, I got up and I talked about Casey. About the sweet boy who grew up to be a remarkable young man. Casey was not always a brave, big soldier man. He was my sweet, sweet baby once. I told the people at the camp named after him that when he was about two years old, he would come up behind me and throw his arms around my legs, kiss me on the butt, and say, "I wuv you mama." I also talked about the loving big brother and wonderful, nearly perfect son. Casey was a regular guy who wanted to get married, have a family, be an elementary school teacher and a deacon in the Catholic Church. He wanted to be a chaplain's assistant in the Army, but was lied to about that also by his recruiter. The last time I talked to him when he called from Kuwait, he was on his way to mass.

For Casey to even join the Army, let alone be killed in battle, was the thing that was most uncharacteristic of him. He was a gentle and kind soul who only wanted to help others. What did his untimely and unnecessary death accomplish? It accomplished reinvigorating a peace movement that was sincere, but not very active—or if active, not well covered by the mainstream media.

Joan sang the song "Joe Hill." In it, Joe Hill says, "I never died." Well, looking out at the faces here at Camp Casey and knowing that for everyone who is present here, there are thousands of others who support our work, I am convinced that Casey never died, and he never will. When I look into the eyes of the kind and gentle souls who have come here, I see Casey and the faces of all the others killed in George Bush's war for greed and profit. We will never forget them, and we will honor them by working for peace.

Joan also sang "Swing Low, Sweet Chariot"—"A thousand angels waiting there for me." I know Casey will be waiting for me when it is my turn, and I know when I finally get there, he's going to hug me and say, "Good job, Mom."

"THANK YOU, MOM. THIS WAS THE BEST DAY OF MY LIFE."

Talk Given at Camp Casey
Wednesday evening, August 24

Isn't she (Joan Baez) amazing? This has been a pretty amazing day.

I was watching Jon Stewart the other night. I haven't watched TV for a long time, and he had Chris Wallace on from Fox News, and they were talking about what's happening out here and they were talking about, well, Cindy's gone, her mom had a stroke, and then they said that Joan Baez gave a concert last night, and Jon Stewart said, "Well, apparently they are trying to stop Vietnam." You know, that kind of offended me, because maybe if we had really stopped Vietnam, Iraq wouldn't have happened. It was such a long struggle after Vietnam—I'm not going to take any credit or blame for this, because I was really young—that it was, like, "Well, we got our troops out now. We don't have to make sure they never do this to our kids again." I am going to make sure that after our troops are brought home from Iraq—and they will be brought back—that we're going to keep the Camp Casey movement going and make sure that our kids are never sent to fight a war for power and greed again.

Probably the country is going to take me at my word from now on. They know I'm not going to give up. It was really hard today when I came in and saw the painting of Casey bigger than life. I miss him so much, and I miss him more every day. But like that song that Joan just sang, "Joe Hill," Casey's not dead. I see him in all of your eyes, and Casey will never die. They can kill the body, but they can't kill the love and the spirit. No matter how hard they try, they can't do that.

I want to tell you about Casey, because this whole movement is because of him and the others who have sacrificed themselves. I don't care about them calling me a crackpot or a tool of the left or a media whore. You know, if I truly was a media whore, do you think I might get myself fixed up a little before coming on stage? These things don't bother me. What bothers me so much is when they say I am dishonoring my son's memory by what I'm doing, that my son would be ashamed of me, or what they'd really like to say, that I'm pissing or shitting or spitting on his grave. Look what Casey has started. I'm here, we're all here, because of Casey and 2000 of our brave young people and tens of thousands of innocent Iraqis. They are behind us, and I see all their faces on your faces.

Casey was a gentle, kind, loving person. He never even got in a fistfight his whole life. Nobody hated him enough to punch him, let alone kill him, and that's what George Bush did. He put our kids in another person's country, and Casey was killed by insurgents. He wasn't killed by terrorists. He was killed by Shiite militia who wanted him out of the country, after Casey had been told he would be welcomed with chocolate and flowers as a liberator. The people of Iraq saw it differently. They saw him as an occupier.

I want you guys to know about Casey. He was an altar boy for ten years, an eagle scout, and an honor student. He was a very brave person who was scared out of his mind on April 4, but he went anyway because he said, "Where my chief goes, I go." But you don't know the little boy.

He used to come up behind me, wrap his arms around my legs, kiss me on the butt, and say, "I wuv you mama." And if he wasn't doing that, he'd walk by and go, "Dinus ha mama," and that meant, "What are you doing mama?" Every night we'd put him to bed. Every night he would say, "Thank you, Mom. This was the best day of my life."

There are a couple of funny stories. Once when he wasn't even two, it was Easter Sunday and we were all at mass, all jammed into one pew, and the church was full, we were standing up singing "The Lamb of God." We were Catholic and we went to kneel down, and as soon as we knelt down, Casey stood up on one of the kneelers and at the top of his voice he goes, "I'm Popeye the sailor man," and everybody in the whole church cracked up. And so from then on, people at our church called him "Popeye." They'd go, "Hey, there goes Popeye."

When he was in kindergarten, he went to the Catholic school where we went to church. He went in the afternoons, and the parking lot was usually full, so we'd have to drive around looking for a place to park. One time, we were driving around and he goes, "Oh mama, there's a place." And I said, "Honey, we can't park there. It's handicapped." And he goes, "Oh, we're not handicapped, we're Catholic."

And then later he thought—you guys who grew up Catholic might understand—that there were only two religions in the world: Catholic and public.

In his rebellious years, when we told him something he didn't agree with, this was the extent of his talking back to us: "Thssst." Seriously, this kid was just an amazing person, and we were so shocked when he joined the Army.

That was the last thing we would have expected from Casey, but also the first thing because he always wanted to help. He always wanted to serve. He thought he was giving something back to his country and community, having been lied to by his recruiter. When I would nurse him, I would promise him that I would never let him go to war. And I broke that promise to him.

This is the boy they say I'm dishonoring by what I do. I know when I get up with Casey, he's gonna say, "Good job, Mom." He's not going to say, "Why'd you make me spin in my grave?" you know. I can just hear him saying, "George Bush, you are really an idiot. You didn't know what you were doing when you killed me. You didn't know what you were getting into." I'm sure Casey's up there with Ken and all the others, and they're just going, "Wow, did these guys have moms? They didn't know that this was going to happen when they killed us?"

Everybody thought Casey would be a priest, but he told me, "Mom I want to get married and have a family." And he wanted to be a deacon in the Catholic Church, which you can be as a married person. His recruiter told him he could be a chaplain's assistant in the Army, but when Casey got there they said, "Well, psych is full. You have to be a cook or a Humvee mechanic." So he became a Humvee mechanic.

He wanted to be an elementary school teacher. He loved kids. He loved animals. He was a very good big brother to Andy, Carly, and Janey. And his murder has left a hole in our hearts and in our family, and it's never going to be replaced. No matter how many wonderful people I meet, how many boys that call me "mom," they're not Casey.

He used to call me every day from Fort Hood. I miss that. For almost a year after he was killed, every time the phone rang I'd think, "Oh that's Casey." It just hits you about fifty times a day that you're never going to talk to him or see him again. That's why I do what I do. I can't bear the thought of another mother having to go through the pain that I'm going through. That's the only reason I do it. That's what we're here for. We're here to make it so our kids' deaths stand for peace and love. This is what Camp Casey is.

And some people are saying, "What are you guys trying to do, re-create the sixties?" as though peace and love are really bad things. They're things that have been missing in our country for decades, and I'm not ashamed to say that this is a place where you can come and feel loved. This is the place where the end of the occupation of Iraq started. This is the place where Americans can come and say, "We've had enough! You might be able to lie to Congress. You might be able to lie to the media. But you're not lying to us anymore." This is it. This is where it has begun, and we're not going stop, ever. We will make sure that this keeps on going. We won't have another war in thirty or forty years and be saying, "Oh, this is another Iraq." It's not going to happen again, ever. And it's not just by me. It's the millions of people who are behind us, making sure that that will happen. And you know when this is going to stop? When the mothers say, "No, I'm not giving my son. I'm not giving my son to you so you can kill him to line your pockets." That's when it's going to stop.

I felt this many times before, just after Casey was born. I looked in his eyes and it seemed he could tell what I was thinking. That's very disarming, when you have like a week-old baby looking at you and you know he knows what you're thinking.

And I knew he was going to be a great man. I just had no idea how great he was going to be or how much it was going to hurt me. So, thank you Casey, and thank you Ken, and thank you all the others. I know they are in heaven, and I know that this movement is growing because we have tens of thousands of angels behind us who are supporting us, saying, "You know, we died, and that was really crappy, but we hope our deaths are going to make the world a better place." It's up to us to make sure that it does. Thank you.

DAY TWENTY
PRESS CONFERENCE
Camp Casey, Thursday morning, August 25

So it was really nice to be here and nice to see, you know, what Casey sacrificed, what Ken sacrificed, what John sacrificed has started in this country, that we are making it stand for peace and not for more killing. I know my son. I know him better than anybody else. And he wasn't married. We were very close. He called me every day when he was at Fort Hood. We talked about all of his life, all of my life, and I lost my best friend when I lost my son. But I know my son, and I know he would say, "I don't want any more of my buddies killed just because I'm dead. I want my buddies to come home alive." And I know when I get up to greet him, when it is my time, he is going to say, "Good job, Mom." He's not going to accuse me of dishonoring his memory. If anybody who knows my son better than me would like to come forward and tell me something different, I will be glad to hear their voices.

Also, my mom. My mom was moved to a private room, and she is doing physical therapy now. Her right side was paralyzed. She had a major stroke, but it wasn't a hemorrhagic stroke, so they are expecting her to at least partially recover, and I want to thank everybody in America for all of their thoughts and prayers. As a matter of fact, everybody from all over the world was praying for my mom. I told my mom she was the most famous stroke victim, you know, at this time. So, she smiled about that. She tried to tell me that she loved me when I left.

And one good thing about Camp Casey and what we started here is that when I left, it didn't end. When I left it thrived and it grew. And it's because I am not alone. I'm not the only one that wants the answers to these questions. There are the people standing behind me here, and there are thousands of military families, hundreds of Gold Star families who want the same answers to the questions. You know, I never, ever got up here and said, "I speak for every single Gold Star family, I speak for every single military family." I've never said that. But I know I speak for thousands of them. I know we speak for thousands of them when we want to know what is the Noble Cause our children died for, what is the noble cause they are still fighting and dying for every day. These are the questions we want the answers to. And there are millions of Americans here with us, thousands here actually in Crawford who want the same answers. They don't have what I like to call skin in the game, but we are all affected. Humanity is affected when one country wages an illegal and immoral war on another country. It affects our entire humanity. And that's why America is behind us, saying we want the answers to those questions, too.

And there are other people who have lost their children who disagree with our position. And I know, with Karen, Melanie, and Susan, we respect their rights to their opinions, because at the end of the day or at the beginning of this quest, we started in the same way, with our loved one coming home in a flag-draped coffin. And if there is any family who says that they believe their child died for a noble cause, I say that is your right if that helps you get through the day, if that helps you in your pain because we all—we might not have the same politics, but trust me, we have the same pain. And we do what we have to do to get through our pain, and we hope they respect us for that, and we respect them in any way they have to do to get through their pain.

Day Twenty

False Freedom Isn't Free

Camp Casey, Thursday, August 25

Today when I was driving back and forth between Camp Casey II and the Crawford Peace House, I saw a lot of signs that say "I'm4W," "Support Our Troops," and the one I hate the most, "Freedom Isn't Free." I am not feeling well tonight, so I am heading to bed before 6 p.m. I have excerpted an article I wrote a few months ago called "A Lie of Historic Proportions."

Iraq has been the tragic Lie of Historic Proportions of Washington, D.C., since before the first Gulf War. For years, Saddam was one of our government's propped-up and militarily supported puppets. Many people have seen the famous footage of Donald Rumsfeld shaking hands with Saddam. I suppose the two are smiling so big for the cameras, because they are kindred spirits. After all of the hand shaking and weapon brokering, when did Saddam become such a bad guy to Bush, Cheney, Halliburton, and Co.? (Insert your favorite reason here.)

During the Clinton regime, the U.S.-UN led sanctions and the weekly bombing raids killed tens of thousands of people in Iraq. Many of them were children, but since one of her children didn't have to be sacrificed to the homicidal war machine, Madeline Albright thinks the slaughter during the "halcyon" Clinton years was "worth it." More lies.

Anyone with even a rudimentary understanding of current events understands that this invasion/occupation of Iraq was not about Saddam being a "bad guy." If that logic is used, then how many innocent Iraqi people have to die before the citizens of America wake up and know that our government is a "bad guy"? We also know that Iraq was not about WMDs. They weren't there and they weren't going to be there for at least a decade, by all reports. Another reason, so wispy and more difficult to disprove, is that America invaded Iraq to bring freedom and democracy to the Iraqi people. When one tries to dispute this particular deception, one is accused of being unpatriotic or hating freedom. Even though correct, the statement "Freedom Isn't Free" is very insulting to me. False freedom is very expensive. Fake freedom costs about two billion of our tax dollars a week. Phony freedom has cost the Iraqi people tens of thousands of innocent lives. Fanciful freedom has meant the destruction of a country and its infrastructure. Tragically, this fabricated notion of freedom and democracy cost me far more than I was willing to pay: the life of my son Casey. The Lie of Historic Proportions also cost me my peace of mind. I do not feel free, and I do not feel like I live in a democracy.

Casey took an oath to protect the U.S. from all enemies "foreign and domestic." He was sent to occupy and die in a foreign country that was no threat to the USA. The biggest threat to our safety, our humanity, and our way of life in America is George and his cronies. Congress made a Mistake of Historic Proportions when it waived its constitutional responsibility to declare war. It is time for the House to make up for that mistake and introduce a resolution of inquiry into the Downing Street Memo.

It is time to put partisan politics behind to do what is correct for once and reclaim America's humanity. It is time for Congress and the American people to work together in peace and justice to rid our country of the stench of greed, hypocrisy, and unnecessary suffering that permeates our White House and our halls of Congress. It is time to hold someone accountable for the carnage and devastation that have been caused. As a matter of fact, it is past time, but it is not too late.

DAY TWENTY-ONE

GEORGE BUSH'S NEW REASON FOR STAYING IN IRAQ

Camp Casey, Friday, August 26

I finally figured out George Bush's *new* reason for staying in Iraq. This reason has also been co-opted by the Move America Forward (forward to what—fascism?) and the poor mothers who would be honored if their sons were killed in George Bush's war for greed and power.

Since the Freedom and Democracy thing is not going so well and the Iraqi parliament is having such a hard time writing a constitution, since violence is mounting against Iraqis and Americans, and since his poll numbers are going down every day, he had to come up with something.

I have continually asked George Bush to quit using Casey's name and the names of the other Gold Star Families for Peace loved ones to justify his continued killing. He continues to say this: "We have to honor the sacrifices of the fallen by completing the mission." So the mission is now this: *We must continue killing Americans because Americans have already been killed!!!*

How can anyone, anyone in their right minds, support this line of reasoning? I have been silent on the Gold Star moms who still support this man and his war by saying that they deserve the right to their opinions because they are in as much pain as I am. I would challenge them, though, at this point to start thinking for themselves. Iraq *did not* have WMDs; Iraq *was not* linked to al Qaeda and 9/11; Iraq *was not* a threat or danger to America. How can these moms who still support George Bush and his insane war in Iraq want more innocent blood shed just because their sons or daughters have been killed? I don't understand it. I don't understand how any mother could want another mother to feel the pain we feel. I am starting to lose a little compassion for them. I know they have been as brainwashed as the rest of America, but they know the pain and heartache, and they should not wish it on another. However, I still feel their pain so acutely and pray for these "continue the murder and mayhem" moms to see the light.

I didn't do my blog last night because I was so exhausted. I am now lying awake at night thinking and worrying about a couple of things. First of all, how can we keep the momentum of Camp Casey going? Our first step is a bus tour consisting of three buses going through three different parts of the country, stopping at various places to do rallies and "visit" Congress members' offices. I had a brainstorm during my press conference yesterday: our first stop will be at Mr. Tom DeLay's office. I just opened my mouth and the words came out, and the bus tour organizers reworked the bus schedule so we could make that happen. But before we even issued the invitation to Tom DeLay, his office had released a statement saying that he was "too busy" to meet with me. In taking Camp Casey to Congress, we are creating problems for the very people who voted to give George the authority to invade an innocent country and cause the deaths of so many people. We will eventually target every congressperson, pro-peace and anti-peace alike, Republican or Democrat, and ask them the same questions we are asking the president. Except with Congress, we are going to add one more thing: "Since there is no Noble Cause, you need to develop a speedy exit strategy and bring our troops home as soon as humanly possible."

The second thing that worries the crap out of me is the almost icon status that I have achieved. I never set out to become the "Rosa Parks of the peace movement." I ventured out on August 6, 2005, to hold George Bush accountable and to raise awareness about his lies and misuse and abuse of power. I didn't set out to become anyone's hero. I am a regular mom who just wants peace and no one else to be murdered for the deceptions of our government. I love the love and support of America; it is what sustains me through these very difficult times and the reich-wing smear campaign. I am blown away and humbled that people are coming from all over the world to meet me and have their pictures taken with me. I am honored when people ask me for my autograph, and I love meeting the little ones. I think we really need to focus our energies on the cause of peace, though—and the message, not the messenger. I am not a perfect person. I am strong, and I do have the *cajones* to tell the world that our "emperor" has no clothes, but it is done out of love of Casey and the others who have died and who are in harm's way, and out of the simple fact that at the end of the day I have to look at myself in the mirror. If I didn't do everything in my power to end this monstrosity of an occupation in Iraq, how could I do that? I promised my boy that I would make the world a better place for his unborn nieces and nephews, and I mean to keep that promise.

We are going to have an eventful day at Camp Casey. We are holding a big rally and so are the pro "continue the killing because Americans have died already" people. I am a little apprehensive about this. We know that the sheriffs know that the other people are coming to stir up trouble and provoke us into violence. Well, that is not going to happen on the Camp Casey side. We will not resort to the same tactics as their leaders.

Camp Casey is a place of peace and love, and we won't let ignorant citizens bring us down. At this point, the smears are amusing me, rather than hurting me.

I will keep you all posted about Saturday's events. Please pray for us that everyone keeps a cool head.

Peace!!!!

DAY TWENTY-TWO
NOT ONE MORE
Camp Casey, Saturday, August 27

A photographer friend of mine went down to Crawford to the Pro-War, Anti-Peace rally today. There were about 1500 people there, he said. He also said that it was the most "Third Reich" spectacle that he had ever seen in America.

My friend said that the speakers were whipping the crowd into a frenzy of hatred for me (like they already didn't hate me?) and for the peace movement. My friend said that the entire theme of the rally was, "Cindy is killing American troops by her anti-American protest." Oh really? Isn't George Bush killing innocent Americans and Iraqis by sending them to fight in an illegal and immoral war for power and greed? I think the real culprit is my neighbor George.

I am really sad that there are still people in America who think that someone exercising her freedom of speech is anti-American. People who say we *don't* have the right to dissent are unpatriotic and un-American. My friend said that the rally was really the scariest thing he had ever seen. Except for one funny part when some people were walking through the crowd with a "Say No to War—Except When a Democrat Is President" (whatever that means???) sign. I guess the people at the rally only read the "Say No to War" part, and they were ripping up the signs and chasing the gentlemen out. The unfortunate sign holders were trying to tell the counter-protesters that they were on Bush's killing side, but the crowd wouldn't hear them.

Our rally had about 2500 people jammed into the Camp Casey II tent. The speakers and music were awesome. Joan sang a few more songs. I told the crowd that I totally understand George Bush's noble cause for continuing the war: I have to kill more Americans because I have already killed so many. Then I posed the question to them that we will pose to Congress and the small minority of Americans (38 to 40 percent) who still believe in George's oil war. How many more lives are you willing to sacrifice before you bring the troops home? I led the crowd in a deafening chant of "Not One More," aimed at George's vacation home.

I kind of feel sorry for George, holed up in his ranch. Not being able to go out unless he flies over in his helicopter. If he drove out of the ranch, he would have to see people who disagree with him. But every time he leaves the ranch now, he faces people demanding answers to the question: What Noble Cause?

George is going golfing in Arizona on Monday and then to San Diego on Monday afternoon and Tuesday. Be sure we will have people in those locations bird-dogging him. He deserves to be made uncomfortable; he is making the entire world more than uncomfortable.

We are relaxing a little bit tonight after the rally. A very nice young man who was wounded and put in a wheel chair by Bush's war on the same day Casey was killed came out tonight. He is spending his honeymoon with his new bride here at Camp Casey. Which reminds me, we are having two weddings here tomorrow: One at Camp Casey I and one at Camp Casey II. We have had so many children and babies come out, too. It is the cycle of life.

I was visited by a second lieutenant from Casey's 2-5 Cavalry who told me to keep up the good work, and Casey's old roommate came out from Fort Hood to meet me. He may have to go back to Iraq soon. He hopes he doesn't have to, since he will be out in six months, but he is pretty sure he will be stop-lossed.

It was so hot today in Crawford. So hot, it seemed like there wasn't enough air to breathe. Then a storm came and gave us some blessed relief.

Update: Some pro-war people came up to Camp Casey II around 10 p.m. and Ann Wright had to call the sheriff, because they were getting a little rowdy.

DAY TWENTY-THREE

IN MY LIFE I LOVED YOU MORE

Camp Casey, Sunday, August 29

Since I began my vigil in Crawford, an average of 2.69 per day of our nation's brave and noble troops have died in Iraq for George's cowardly and ignoble war; 2.69 families per day have been devastated for no reason except that we have to continue killing American soldiers because so many have been killed already. My heart and soul go out to these families who had a loved one killed so needlessly and avoidably.

How many more are we as Americans going to tolerate before we force the reckless commander-in-chief to bring our kids home? How much more blood are we going to allow Congress to wash their hands in before we force them to force George to bring our children home?

We are doing everything at Camp Casey to build awareness of this illegal and immoral occupation of Iraq. Now we need your help. We are taking Camp Casey to Congress. We plan to hold rallies and meetings in key congressional districts (Democratic and Republican alike) where the incumbent is weak on the war. Here is the letter I am sending to all of our congressional representatives:

DEAR [REPRESENTATIVE],

My son Casey, just 24, was killed in Baghdad on April 4, 2004. It is devastating to me knowing that Casey died needlessly, that so many other families face this same grief, and that new families are added daily. I have been sitting outside President Bush's ranch in Crawford since August 6 in a roadside ditch we named Camp Casey, seeking a meeting and answers to our questions about this immoral war. I have been joined there by other mothers and families, many of whom have lost children in the war, some who have children now serving in the military, and still others who in one way or another have been touched by the war.

The president has not been willing to meet with me, but he must meet and listen to you. President Bush sent our sons and daughters to war in Iraq. Congress gave him the authority to do so. That's why we are now turning to you, the elected officials who have the power to declare wars—and end wars. We come to you with grieving hearts to request that you meet with us to answer our simple questions:

President Bush has said that brave Americans like my son Casey have died for a "noble cause." What is that "noble cause"?

How many more lives are we as a country willing to sacrifice in Iraq? How many are you personally willing to sacrifice?

What are you specifically doing to bring our sons and daughters home from this needless war?

Mothers from your district—all of whom share my conviction that this war must come to an end—are eager to meet with you and pose to you the questions that the president has refused to answer for me. They will be coming to meet you with a symbol from our vigil in Crawford and will seek honest, straightforward responses to our simple questions. They are your constituents, and they will be asking you my questions, their questions, and the nation's questions. They are going to ask you, your colleagues, and the president to answer us.

As a member of Congress, you have the enormous responsibility to end this tragedy and bring our sons and daughters home now. Meet with us, answer us, and show us that there need not be a Camp Casey in your district. Show us that the Crawford Camp Casey, brought on by a stonewalling leader, was all we need. Show us your compassion and leadership.

Sincerely,
CINDY SHEEHAN
MOTHER OF CASEY SHEEHAN

Today was extraordinary at Camp Casey. It was filled with love, passion, and compassion. We started off the day with a prayer service led by religious leaders of all faiths, topped off with a little preaching by the Reverend Al Sharpton, who gave an amazing talk in support of Camp Casey and all we are doing. Right before the Reverend Sharpton arrived, Sean Hannity said that if he were truly a man of God, instead of supporting me the reverend would "denounce" me for speaking ill of the president. The reverend didn't take Hannity's advice, and I am glad.

The next stunning event was the marriage of Peter and Genevieve at Camp Casey II. It was so beautiful. Genevieve walked down the aisle toward Peter and his two sons while we all hummed "Here Comes the Bride." The couple for peace then had a collection taken up for our bus tour, in lieu of gifts. They also made a generous donation to the tour. It was amazing, beautiful, and touching, and I am so honored, but not surprised, that they chose to begin their new lives together in such a loving place as Camp Casey. At the end of the ceremony, they played "In My Life," by the Beatles. One part of the song says, "Some are dead and some are living, in my life, I loved you more." I had about all I could handle when I heard that line, and I wept for my loss but also for my gain. Camp Casey has given me back my joy for life and a renewed sense of hope for my future and my country's future.

We ended the day reciting a rosary, led by Martin Sheen. Martin said Camp Casey was "holy ground," and he met with the Iraq veterans and with me. I called him my "dream president." I am so happy that at least I was able to meet with a president, if a TV one, who turns out to be a very nice guy on top of everything.

Just another day at Camp Casey.

DAY TWENTY-FIVE

GOODBYE TO CRAWFORD, BUT NOT TO CAMP CASEY

Camp Casey, Tuesday, August 30

While George golfed yesterday, the worst hurricane ever struck New Orleans, oil went up to over $68 a barrel, and an American soldier was killed in the charade and cataclysmic occupation of Iraq. The soldier's family doesn't even know what's going to hit them yet. The death is "Pending Notification." I continually ask myself, "How do George Bush and other deathmongers live with themselves?" While George vacations and bikes and golfs his way to the lowest poll numbers since Richard Nixon, other "patriots" are wrapping themselves in the stars and stripes and going along with the farce that the mission from hell, "killing more people in Iraq because so many have already been killed," is somehow a good thing ordained by God. I can live with myself, but trust me, sleep does not come easily to me these days.

Yesterday at Camp Casey was again, naturally, an amazing day. Dennis Banks, from the American Indian Movement, came with a group of Native American musicians, and they made a presentation to me. He gave me a shawl in the tradition of Tecumseh, and he pinned a brooch of five stars on it, from "one chief to another." He also said we should all change our last names to Sheehan, and he will be known as Dennis Banks Sheehan! Sheehan is Gaelic for "Peace," which I think is such a cool thing, and not a coincidence. Casey Sheehan's sacrifice will stand for peace forever.

I missed the candlelight vigil at Camp Casey I last night, but I heard that the counter-protestors came over and held vigil with us for our killed heroes. I heard it was beautiful and life-affirming. This is what Camp Casey does for us: it transforms bitter anger into righteous, productive anger. It turns hate into love. It brings people together in new love and cements mature relationships. It brings other people together who would normally not ever meet and makes them lifelong soul-friends. It heals broken hearts and mends broken souls. I know Camp Casey has healed my broken soul and heart. A veteran from the Iraq tragedy told me that he is now cured of any bad feelings he had.

Just another day at Camp Casey.

I must admit when I sat down in the ditch on August 6, I thought to myself, "Self, what the hell did you do? Texas in August? A ditch filled with fire ants, rattlesnakes, and chiggers? Pooping in a bucket? Dodging lightning bolts and heat exhaustion?" But I knew I would have to suffer it through to the end. I knew that the people of Iraq and our soldiers have it far worse than we did. I thought that as long as I could have plenty of water and an occasional shower at the Peace House, I would survive.

What I never thought, however, was that I would grow to love it here, that I would be so overwhelmed by the magnitude of love and support I received that I would be depressed to leave Camp Casey. I don't want to leave, but I know that for the Camp Casey movement to keep growing, we have to leave Crawford and take Camp Casey to the people.

Tonight I will write to look back on the good times, the less-than-good times, and the miracles that occurred here in Crawford. But I want to thank one person for the best "vacation" and most amazing experience I have ever had—George Bush. Thank you, George, for not meeting with me on August 6, and thank you for being the motivation for Camp Casey. I know you don't want Camp Casey to come to the place you reside between vacations, so I would suggest you bring our troops home immediately.

But most of all, thank you my son. Thank you for living the kind of life that inspires people to work for peace and justice. Thank you for choosing me to be your mom. Thank you for being the embodiment of love, and thank you for being the inspiration for the Camp Casey movement. I promise you it won't end until all of your buddies are brought home. And I promise I will fight for your unborn nieces and nephews and the rest of the children of the world, so they won't be misused and abused by corrupt leadership like you and your buddies were.

I love you, Casey.

DAY TWENTY-SIX

MY LAST POST FROM CRAWFORD

Camp Casey, Wednesday, August 31

"If Zarqawi and bin Laden gain control of Iraq, they would create a new training ground for future terrorist attacks. They'd seize oil fields to fund their ambitions. They could recruit more terrorists by claiming an historic victory over the United States and our coalition." —George Bush, August 30, 2005, in San Diego

So it is official. Casey had his blood shed in Iraq for Oil.

He died so we could pay over $3.00 a gallon for gas. Like I suspected all along, my dear, sweet son, almost 1900 others, and tens of thousands of innocent Iraqis died so the oil fields wouldn't "fall into the hands of terrorists," and so George and his immoral band of greedy robber barons could become wealthier. Like I have said all along, how can these people sleep at night and how can they choke down their food knowing it is purchased off of the flesh and blood of others? We have found our "Noble Cause." And it is Oil. This man and his handlers need to be stopped.

Well, George and I are leaving Crawford today. George is finished playing golf and telling his fables in San Diego, so he will be heading to Louisiana to see the devastation that his environmental policies and his killing policies have caused. Recovery would be easier and much quicker if more than half of the National Guard members in the three states involved weren't in Iraq and nearly all of the National Guard's equipment. Plus, with the two billion dollars a week that the private contractors are siphoning from our treasury, how are we going to pay for helping our own citizens in Louisiana, Mississippi, and Alabama? And should I dare say "global warming?" and be branded as a "conspiracy theorist" on top of everything else the right-wingers say about me?

We are now packing up Camp Casey and leaving Crawford and heading to George's place of employment. He wouldn't talk to us, his employers, while we were here to give him his "job evaluation," so we must go to him to have our little chat.

I just want to thank a few people and groups for their support, help, and love while we have been here in Crawford. So many people made the Camp Casey experience possible and so successful. If I miss someone, I am so sorry. That is the difficult thing about thanking people. I love you all, even if I don't remember to thank you!!

My sister, Dede Miller: My kids' second mom who is always by my side and supports me 100 percent in whatever I do. My cause is her cause, and I couldn't do what I do without her.

Carly, Andy, and Janey: Who would love to see more of their mom, but who understand that we are trying to save their future by what we do. I love you guys, and I will see you very, very soon (yea!!). I couldn't do what I do without their love and support.

The Crawford Peace House: I got an e-mail from Hadi Jawad the day that I decided to come and camp in Crawford, and he pledged the help and support of the Peace House. At that time, they only had a few bucks in their checking account and the phone was turned off. Now, thanks to America, they have been able to keep Camp Casey going, and they will be able to continue their good works indefinitely. Thanks to John Wolf who had the vision for peace in Crawford, and I think that Camp Casey was a fulfillment of his vision. They are going to make a garden and call it "The Casey Sheehan Memorial Peace Garden." What a tribute to my son.

Code Pink: Jodie Evans and Tiffany and Alicia were the first ones here on Monday 08/08 to jump in and save me from going crazy and hopping on one of the trains that runs past the Peace House and pulling an Agatha Christie. Code Pink also worked tirelessly (and I mean tirelessly) outside of Camp Casey.

MoveOn and True Majority: For organizing the highly successful candlelight vigils.

Lisa Fithian: For all the organizing work she did behind the scenes.

Gold Star Families for Peace, Iraq Veterans Against the War, Military Families Speak Out, and Veterans for Peace: Our organizations with "skin in the game," for all of their support, presence, love, and help.

Bill Mitchell: Bill's son Mike was KIA in the same battle as Casey, and he was the first Gold Star Families for Peace member to come to Camp Casey and take some of the heat off of me. He found a new love at Camp Casey (one of our miracles), and I am so-o-o happy about that. Plus, Bill is one of my most ardent supporters, and he just gets in the middle of things, digs in, and helps wherever. I love him, and he and his family will be part of our family forever.

Fred Mattlage: For donating the amazing piece of land for our use that allowed Camp Casey to expand to include thousands.

Air America: The *Morning Sedition*, Randi Rhodes, Mike Malloy, and Laura Flanders. Thank you for your support. Ed Schultz belongs there, too, although he is not affiliated with Air America Radio. Amy Goodman was here, too!

The bloggers on The Daily Kos and most bloggers in general (see "Resources for Action and Education" at the end of this book): I would read their comments every day after I posted my diary, and I was always heartened and encouraged by their remarks. After all of the negativity, their positivity gave me strength to go on. In addition, the first night we were in Crawford and being harassed, they were posting things and getting the word out that we were there alone and defenseless, which may have saved our lives, or saved us from being injured or harassed out of there.

So many other people: The Camp Casey volunteers—literally hundreds. The more than 10,000 people who came through Camp Casey. Ann Wright who kept Camp Casey going. Arianna Huffington for her advice and support. Joan Baez who kept Camp Casey's spirits alive while I was in California attending to my sick mother. George Bush for not meeting with me on August 6. Martin Sheen for his support and presence. The American Indian Movement for Dennis Banks and Russell Means. Gary Hart, John Conyers, Maxine Waters, Barbara Lee, Sheila Jackson Lee, Jan Schakowsky, Dennis Kucinich, Frank Pallone, Lynn Woolsey, Chuck Hagel, Ralph Nader, Jim McDermott, Walter Jones, Charlie Rangel, and the other politicos who either came to Camp Casey or called me to offer their support and love. I know I am forgetting some, but thanks to you all. Joe Wilson and his family for paving the way for me to be able to ignore and dismiss the right-wing smear machine, who always tried to marginalize and discredit me by exaggerating or twisting my words and lying about me. The clergy who were there with their love and support: Rabbi Arthur Waskow, Rabbi Dennis

Shulman, Rev. Al Sharpton, Rev. Bob Edgars, Rev. Jesse Jackson (who prayed bedtime prayers with me), Rita Brock, etcetera.

There were so many good people who donated money, goods, or services who want to be kept anonymous.

But especially to Americans who resonated with Camp Casey and gave us prayers, support, money, love, and, most of all, hope for the future.

We will take our country back. And it will be a country that we want back.

God Bless America!!!!

ANTI-WAR PROTESTS
NEAR BUSH RANCH END

By Angela K. Brown
The Associated Press

Wednesday, August 31, 2005

Crawford, Texas— As anti-war activist Cindy Sheehan's protest outside President Bush's ranch comes to an end, her supporters are embarking on a three-week bus tour of the country to continue rallying people against the war in Iraq. The "Bring Them Home Now Tour" stops in Dallas and Austin Wednesday as it winds its way to a planned march in Washington, D.C., on September 26.

Sheehan, who had pledged to remain at her Crawford camp for Bush's entire monthlong vacation unless he agreed to meet with her, said Tuesday she's glad Bush never showed up to discuss her son's death in Iraq because his absence "galvanized the peace movement."

"I look back on it, and I am very, very, very grateful he did not meet with me, because we have sparked and galvanized the peace movement," she said. "If he'd met with me, then I would have gone home, and it would have ended there."

Sheehan and about 50 other peace activists arrived in Crawford August 6, the day after she spoke at a Veterans for Peace convention in Dallas. She and a few others spent that night in chairs in ditches, without food or flashlights, off the main road leading to the president's ranch.

Two top Bush administration officials talked to Sheehan the first day, but the president never did, although he has said that he sympathizes with her and acknowledged her right to protest. His vacation is to end Wednesday, two days early, so he can monitor federal efforts to help victims of Hurricane Katrina on the Gulf Coast.

Sheehan's vigil attracted crowds of other anti-war demonstrators. Most stayed a few hours or days at the original roadside camp or at the second, larger site about a mile away on a private lot offered by a sympathetic landowner.

The massive response has transformed her life, she said.

"I thought nobody cared about our children killed in the war, but millions care, and millions care about our country and want to make it better," she said. "The love and support I've received give me hope that my life can someday be normal."

The protest also sparked counter-rallies by Bush supporters who accused Sheehan of using her son's death to push the liberal agenda of groups supporting her. Critics also said the protest was hurting U.S. troop morale in Iraq.

Sheehan will leave the tour next week to spend time with her mother who recently suffered a stroke, causing Sheehan to miss a week of the protest in Crawford. She plans to attend the march in the nation's capital, hoping to reunite with people she met on the Texas roadside that became known as "Camp Casey," after her son.

"When I first started here, I was sitting in the ditch thinking, 'What the heck did I do? Texas in August, the chiggers, fire ants, rattlesnakes, uncomfortable accommodations'—but I'm going to be sad leaving here," Sheehan said. "I hope people will say that the Camp Casey movement sparked a peace movement that ended the war in Iraq."

V.

THE
BRING THEM
HOME NOW
BUS TOUR

Crawford, Texas, to Washington, D.C.
September 1–26, 2005

I hate to be harsh, but we're not
accepting any excuses for not bringing our
troops home now.

How Does Scotty McClellan Live with Himself?

Thursday, September 1

Yesterday, we left Camp Casey and it was very emotional for me. I never imagined I would feel so badly about leaving Crawford, Texas, behind. But I never counted on the Crawford, Texas, experience turning into the Camp Casey experience. We actually walked around most of the time with stupid grins on our faces, because being at Camp Casey was such a happy experience. Now we are carrying Camp Casey to the nation.

I left on the same bus I'd pulled up in—The Veterans for Peace Impeachment Tour Bus. It was excruciatingly hot as we rolled into Austin—100-plus-degree heat with no air. Even before we got off Interstate 35, our bus was greeted by honks, waves, and cheers from our fellow rush-hour motorists. I was afraid we would cause an accident in the go-sometimes-but-mostly-stopped traffic.

We arrived safely at Congressman Lloyd Doggett's office and spoke to his aide. It was a great meeting, and we are 100 percent behind Lloyd Doggett, and he is 100 percent behind us. From the Congressman's office, we went to the state capitol, and I received a Texas flag and a proclamation welcoming me to Texas from an Austin state legislator. Since I'd been in

Texas for nearly a month, it felt nice to finally be welcomed. Then we marched to Austin City Hall holding a "Support Our Troops, Bring Them Home Now" banner, with hundreds of people following us. We sang and chanted as we walked, and people were joining us from the sidewalks. It was the most remarkable march I've ever been a part of.

At City Hall, we were greeted by more than two thousand people! I joked about moving to Austin and running for mayor. Many in the crowd had been to Camp Casey at one time or another. David Rovics played a couple of songs, including "Every Mother's Son," about Casey, and then Jim Hightower spoke. It is always a treat to hear him.

I spoke next, and I talked about how George couldn't come out and see me when I was in Crawford, because he didn't have an answer for me. There is no "Noble Cause," so how could he answer me? He admitted the other day that it was for oil. I don't consider that a good enough reason for so many people being dead. Iraq could and would sell us their oil. I really believe immoral criminals are running our country, and it is making me even more determined to save it with millions of my fellow citizens' help.

This morning, I was watching Scotty McClellan's press conference, and the press corps was asking him about the failure in preparations for the hurricane. He kept on saying, "This is not the time to point fingers, lay blame, or for politics." Of course it isn't, when the blame lies squarely on the shoulders of the people he works for. From diverting money to Iraq that was intended to shore up the levees and make New Orleans safer, to sending 70 percent of the National Guard from Louisiana, Mississippi, and Alabama to Iraq in a war that never has made sense, George Bush has failed this country. By his actions in the first few days of the Katrina tragedy, he has further demonstrated that he doesn't care about Americans whether they are in Iraq or in America.

We on the Bring Them Home Now Bus Tour really agonized if we should continue the trip, considering what was going on in our country. We came to the conclusion that it was more important for us to "stay the course" and point out the failures of this administration and how this illegal occupation of Iraq is making our country far less safe than it was before. We decided to "complete the mission" to honor the sacrifices of our fallen heroes, to strive and not give up until our troops are brought home from Iraq and everyone in both countries is more secure.

Tom DeLay's aide said he probably won't meet with me because I don't "comport" myself properly. I told him that we don't think Tom DeLay "comports" himself properly, and I could probably get a meeting if Casey had a feeding tube in him instead of being dead for his boss's support of a horrible war.

His aide said he didn't know what I was referring to. When are these people going to stop thinking I am stupid?

Dangerous Incompetence

Saturday, September 3

George Bush has been an incompetent failure his entire life. Fortunately, for humanity, he was just partying his way through school, running companies into the ground, and being an alcoholic and cocaine abuser for most of that time, and his incompetence was limited to hurting the people who worked for him and his own family. The people in his life who were hurt by his incompetence probably have been able to "get on" with their lives. Now, though, his incompetence affects the world and is responsible for so many deaths and so much destruction. How many of us did not foresee the mess he would make of the world when he was selected the first time? We saw what he had done to Texas. How many of us marveled and were so discouraged and amazed when he was "re-elected"? We saw what he had done to the world. Dangerous incompetence should never be rewarded, let alone be rewarded so handsomely as in George's case.

The Camp Casey Movement has been struggling with how best we can help the government-ravaged people of New Orleans and the surrounding areas. We sent a busload of supplies into Covington, Louisiana, which is a poor, African-American town across Lake Pontchartrain from New Orleans. I had the privilege of visiting Covington with my friends Buddy and Annie Spell last July. It was a community filled with love and laughter.

The Bring Them Home Now Tour bus that went into Covington is the Veterans for Peace Impeachment Tour bus that I rode on into and out of Crawford. They took about 10,000 pounds of leftover Camp Casey supplies, and we had two trucks filled to the brim with leftover water that we got into Covington. The tour bus also has satellite internet and a satellite phone and is the only communications that Covington has with the outside world.

Following is an email that our tour received from Gordon, one of the bus drivers who bravely drove to Covington. I've left it intact, without editing:

I can't recommend coming here but, if you must, we do need help! During the day we are going out into the community with water and baby supplies lunch foods. But, there has been an attack on the Armory and the cops are scared. We have move into Covington middle school and we are giving the red cross our assistance with medical supplies and food services. Until we arrived, they only had MRE's (Meals Ready To Eat). They just brought in 5 new borns babies from the hospital as they are expecting more casualties, We brought in a generator and solar powered lights, no power, no phone service here, our satellite link is the only connection to the outside. The Marshal Law enforcement that will be coming to New Orleans with the Army, could create mass panic that will lead to more refugees, we have twenty right now and room for 100. Don't come here unless you are prepared to work!.

I should say, stay out on the road and raise money for the relief effort. But make up your own minds.

We need to keep the public aware of what is going on here and all over SOLA (Southern Louisiana).

If you want to help go an established refugee camp and provide your internet access to document who is there and what they plan to do to the website. Use your satellites access to maximize the story of the relief effort!

GORDON

There it is.

We will finish the tour so we can talk about what an abject failure this administration is. The unnecessary tragedy in New Orleans is directly related to the unnecessary tragedy in Iraq, "unnecessary" being the operative word.

Innocent people are dying daily in this world. In the crush of the hurricane story, the fact that 950 people (mostly women and children) were trampled to death in Iraq was buried in the back pages of the newspapers. Those are 950 people who would still be alive if George Bush were not president. Nine hundred fifty people in Iraq plus how many in the Gulf States died while the emperor strummed a guitar and knocked a golf ball around? And eight of our brave and wonderful soldiers have needlessly been killed in Iraq since Monday.

I really believe that George and his band of incompetent and dangerous thugs need to resign. It would be the only honorable and competent thing to do.

HOW MANY MORE INNOCENT PEOPLE ARE THEIR GREED AND INDIFFERENCE GOING TO TAKE DOWN WITH THEM?

Friday, September 9

After a few days' rest, I am heading back out on the Truth Trail. Camp Casey III in Covington, Louisiana, is really hopping. Members of our group took ten thousand pounds of supplies from Camp Casey I and II to Covington, a poor African-American town.

The Vets for Peace bus is doubling as the communications center, since it has satellite internet and a satellite phone. Members of Code Pink from Austin and Houston collected clothes, baby formula, and diapers and delivered them to Camp Casey III. The situation is dire, and we are glad that we can provide some of our fellow Americans with the basic comforts of home that our government is not supplying to them. We are putting our money, time, and energy into helping the people of Louisiana. Because of the misplaced priorities of the administration, these people have become the collateral damage of the occupation of Iraq.

I was stunned at the level of corruption, incompetence, and callousness exhibited by this administration toward the Katrina disaster. How many more innocent people are we going to let their greed and indifference take down with them?

During the Bring Them Home Now Tour, we are going to ask members of Congress: 1) What Noble Cause are our children fighting for, dying for, and killing for in Iraq? 2) What are our elected officials doing to end the occupation of Iraq? 3) How many more innocent Iraqis and Americans are we willing to sacrifice?

Should be an interesting trip. I'll keep you posted.

"MEET WITH THE MOMS"
HALLS OF FAME AND SHAME

Sunday, September 11

Today as we honor and memorialize our countrymen and women tragically killed on 9/11, we must honor their memories by working to hold this dangerously incompetent administration accountable and responsible for its continuing devastation of our country.

Since Wednesday, I have been meeting with Congressmembers and speaking at rallies with hundreds and hundreds of people. We had a rally in front of Congressman Denny Hastert's office in Batavia, Illinois, but we didn't get a meeting. He will go on our "Meet with the Moms Hall of Shame," along with Tom DeLay, whose aide at least spoke to us on the phone, even if it was nonproductive.

I met with an aide to Dianne Feinstein in San Francisco. The Senator will also go on our Hall of Shame. Her aides—I have only spoken with her aides, even though I have requested three meetings with her—have admitted that she knows that Iraq was a mistake and if she knew then what she knows now, she never would have given George Bush the authority to invade and occupy Iraq. First of all, I don't buy that argument. Anyone with a brain knew George was lying in the insane rush to the invasion of Iraq, and second of all, if she believes it is a mistake, then she should be working to bring our troops home. Casey and so many tens of thousands of others should still be alive, and humanity is damaged immensely by allowing this travesty to continue. The aide we spoke to, James Molinari, was pretty defensive and borderline rude when he spoke to me, a Gold Star sister, Dr. Nooshin Razani, and a member of Military Families Speak Out, Anne Roesler. Anne's son,

Michael, is in Iraq for his third tour of duty. As we all know, not one Senator, Congressperson, or member of Bush's criminal administration has any loved one serving any Iraq.

These are Mrs. Feinstein's cardboard hurdles that must be jumped over before we bring our troops home. (Again, I feel her aide was patronizing us and making the mistake of assuming that if we are women, who are obviously distraught because we have had horrible losses and potential horrible losses, then we must not know what we are talking about.)

1. IRAQ NEEDS A CONSTITUTION.

The constitution that Iraq is working on is one that will create a theocracy and an Islamic republic that will deny women in Iraq the rights that they had before the U.S. invaded their country. It will make the region less stable than it is now and was before.

2. IRAQ NEEDS LEADERSHIP.

Puppet leadership with the neocons pulling the strings. Leaders like Ahmed Chalabi, who is a CIA-trained operative who had everything to gain politically and monetarily by toppling the Hussein regime.

3. ENOUGH IRAQI SOLDIERS NEED TO BE TRAINED.

These poor unfortunate souls are not going to be trained in Iraq. They are seen as collaborators and are targets of the insurgents. I often wonder how desperate the Iraqis must be for jobs if they are willing to risk their lives standing in line for a job application.

4. IRAQ MUST HAVE INFRASTRUCTURE.

This infrastructure will not be built and maintained properly with our military presence in Iraq.

We pointed out all of these counter-arguments out to Mr. Molinari. I also asked whether the senator, as a mother and grandmother, would be willing to sacrifice one of her loved ones so people can line their pockets with her children's blood. At this point, I don't believe that Dianne Feinstein represents her constituents, the people of California, of which I am one. Not only is she weak on the Iraq issue, she introduced Condi ("smoking gun") Rice for her confirmation hearing, and she called John (Death Squad) Negroponte "a great public servant." If she refuses to be a leader on getting our troops out of Iraq, then we the people of California need to withdraw our support of her.

On a better note, I spoke with Senator Barbara Boxer, also from California. We Golden Staters are so proud of our other Senator. She is one hundred percent behind us and one hundred percent on board with bringing the troops home from this nightmare. She also questioned the stuffing out of Condi at her confirmation hearings. Our beloved Mrs. Boxer could be elected Queen of California. I wish Mrs. Feinstein would exercise real leadership like Mrs. Boxer and quit pandering to the center and to special interests.

Another bright spot in my Congressional talks was Nancy Pelosi from San Francisco, the house minority leader. I had, up until last Friday, been very disappointed with the lack of leadership that I saw that she was exhibiting on this war. Our talk was very productive, and she is, I believe, willing to take a new leadership role in bringing our troops home from this quagmire. She said it was because of the leadership that I have shown by going down and challenging the Emperor that more House Dems will grow backbones and challenge the President and his lies.

Lloyd Dogget of Austin, Texas, Henry Waxman of Los Angeles, Maxine Waters of Los Angeles, and Cynthia McKinney of Georgia will also go up on our "Hall of Fame" list. Maxine and Cynthia have always been strong critics of the invasion and occupation of Iraq, and Mr. Waxman is coming around to our side in a big way. I am meeting with Frank Pallone of New Jersey on Monday, and he has already told me we will work together to get our young men and women out of harm's way asap. Congressman Charles Rangel of New York was the first to answer our questions and go on our Hall of Fame list. Senator Jeff Bingaman from New Mexico joins Senator Boxer on our Hall of Fame. Welcome Senator Bingaman and thank you!

The Bring Them Home Now Bus Tour had a great rally in Atlanta last night. Hundreds of people came to the Victory Church to hear Gold Star Moms from Georgia, Gold Star Families for Peace members, Military Families Speak Out members, and an Iraq war vet share our war stories. Congresswoman McKinney informed us that she spoke the "I" word (impeachment) on the house floor the other day, and she got a standing ovation from the crowd.

It is a potentially devastating time in our nation's history. Either we will kick out the criminally negligent leaders who have raped our country of its integrity, lifeblood, and treasure, and once again have a country we can be proud of; or we will allow the madmen to continue to take us down the path of destruction. I vote for taking our country back, and I think that is the direction we are going. With the grassroots help of our fellow citizens and with continuing to hold Congress accountable and pressuring them to do the right thing, we are on the right track. We need to show our elected leaders that we, as patriotic Americans, mean business.

I am deeply appreciative to Michael Moore and MichaelMoore.com for the continuing support of Camp Caseys I and II and especially for his support of Camp Casey III and his tireless work to bring supplies and hope to the people of Louisiana who have been all but abandoned by their government. Thank you to the readers of MichaelMoore.com for your generous response and support of all of the Camp Caseys, also. We are so encouraged and heartened by the efforts of true Americans to take our country back.

A BRIGHT SPOT IN BUSH WORLD, AMID MISERABLE FAILURES ON THE SAME PLANET

Tuesday, September 13

It has been one month and one week since I sat in a ditch in Crawford, Texas. I can hardly believe it. So much has happened, and at the same time, so little.

I arrived at Camp Casey III in Covington, Louisiana, today, after getting up at 3 a.m. yesterday to head for the airport. I was prepared to be shocked by what I saw in Louisiana, but one can never fully prepare for such devastation and tragedy. After living in a country your entire life it is so difficult to see callous indifference on such an immense scale. When I reflect on how the mother of the imbecile who is running our country said that the people in the Astrodome are happy to be there, it angers me beyond comparison. Many of the people in Louisiana who were displaced have nice, if modest homes that are perfectly fine. I wonder why the government made them leave at great expense and uproot families who have been living in their communities for generations.

After arriving at Camp Casey III, we took the Veterans for Peace Impeachment Tour Bus into New Orleans. The stench and the destruction here are unbelievable. I've seen hurricane zones in the Florida panhandle, but nothing could have prepared me for this.

I saw in the paper that George Bush said the recovery in the Gulf States would be "hard work." That's what he said about sending troops to Iraq and looking at the casualty reports every day: "It's hard work." That man has never known a day of hard work in his life. The people on the ground in Covington scoffed at George's little junket to Louisiana yesterday. He stayed in the French Quarter and a ward that weren't even damaged. The Veterans for Peace took me to Algiers, Louisiana, on the West Bank. The part of Algiers we went to was very poor and black. The people of Algiers know what hard work is.

Algiers had no flooding. All the damage was from winds. Trees got knocked over, shingles flew off roofs, signs were blown over, and a dead body was lying on the ground for two weeks before someone came to get it. Still, Algiers came through Katrina relatively unscathed. I don't understand why our federal government tried to force the people out of the community. Malik Rahim, a new friend and a resident of Algiers, told us stories of the days after the hurricane. The government declared martial law but had no effective police presence to enforce it. Malik said the lawlessness was rampant. People were running out of food and water. Although their homes were pretty intact and what they wanted was to stay and have food and water brought to them, they were being forced to go to the Superdome. The town of 76,000 people dwindled down to 3,000.

The diehards were rewarded last Wednesday when the Veterans for Peace rolled into town with food and water. The Camp Casey III people were the first ones to bring any relief to Algiers. Our government—the people who are supposed to look after its citizens—failed them.

In two short weeks, Malik and his community have opened a clinic that also serves as a food-and-supply distribution center, and they are planning to open two more. Malik has set up a communications center for the community to use, in an apartment near his house. They have a saying, "Not Charity, Solidarity." All the aid in Algiers is driven by the needs of the community.

The residents of Algiers desperately needed help and hope before the hurricane. When I think of how many other poor neighborhoods are being decimated and made so desperate and hopeless by the failed policies of the Bush administration, it makes me so angry. But when I see what the people of Algiers are doing to help themselves, and what the people of America are doing to help them help themselves, it gives me hope. Algiers can be a model for all our communities.

One thing that really troubled me during my visit to Louisiana was the level of military presence. I had imagined that if the military was to be used in a CONUS (Continental U.S.) operation, they would be there to help clothe, feed, shelter, and protect the citizens. But what I saw was an occupied city. Soldiers were walking around in patrols of seven, with their weapons slung on their backs. Sandbags that had been taken from private property were used to make machine gun nests. I wanted to ask what it would take for one of them to shoot me.

The vast majority of people who were looting in New Orleans were doing so to feed their families or get resources to get their families out of there. If I had a store with an inventory of insured belongings and a tragedy happened, I would fling my doors open and tell everyone to take what they need. It is only stuff. When our fellow citizens are told to "shoot to kill" other fellow citizens because they want to stay alive, that is military and governmental fascism gone out of control. What I saw today in Algiers lifted up my spirits, but what I also saw today in Algiers frightened me terribly.

The failure at every level of our government is criminal negligence. Tens of thousands of families in our country have been devastated because of the incompetence and callousness of our so-called leadership. And at the same time, Americans are stepping up to the plate to help each other. And now we need to step up to the plate to hold George accountable for the abominations in Iraq and Louisiana. George has taught us that we are self-sufficient and that we have a country that is worth fighting for. We are not going away.

I hear that Pat Boone, on a conservative radio talk show in San Francisco, told the listeners that after we stole the supplies from the Red Cross, we gave them to the enemies of America who are like the people who want to fly airplanes into our buildings. Boone said that we were giving supplies to enemies of America, because we were distributing the supplies from a mosque. First of all, accusing me of stealing is slander, and second, we were helping Americans. Just because their government abandoned them, we shouldn't feed them and give them medicine and supplies? I thought Pat Boone was supposed to be a Christian man? Third, isn't freedom of religion one of our constitutional guarantees?

It is a Christ-like principal to feed the hungry, clothe the naked, and shelter the homeless. That's what is happening in Algiers and other places in Louisiana, but by the people of America, not the so-called "Christians" in charge. If George Bush truly listened to God and read the words of the Christ, Iraq and the devastation in New Orleans would have never happened.

I don't care if a human being is black, brown, white, yellow or pink. I don't care if a human being is Christian, Muslim, Jewish, Buddhist, or pagan. I don't care what flag a person salutes. If a human being is hungry, it is up to another human being to feed him or her. George Bush needs to stop talking, admit the mistakes of his failed administration, pull our troops out of occupied New Orleans and Iraq, and excuse himself from power. The only way America will become more secure is when we have a new administration that cares about all Americans and not just the top two percent of the wealthiest.

WE REALLY SUPPORT THE TROOPS

Friday, September 16

All three legs of the Camp Casey to D.C. tour are going very well! We have three RVs going from city to city, and we are speaking to hundreds, sometimes thousands of people, receiving positive responses from all over America with amazingly little opposition. Today in Raleigh, North Carolina, at the university, there were some Young Republicans who support the president and support the war. I tried to get one of the many military recruiters on campus to go over and sign them up, but they wouldn't even look at me. The recruiters are missing a golden opportunity to swell their ranks. I had a feeling, though, that the Young killing supporters wouldn't be willing to go over and put their money where their mouths are. One of the fine American baby chicken hawks told a member of our tour whose brother was killed in Iraq that someone has to stay in school and employ people. Sounds like the Dick Cheney alternative to serving your country.

The people on the three RVs are true Americans serving their country without reservation. Most of the patriots on the tour gave their entire months of August to be at Camp Casey in Crawford, and now they are giving their Septembers to be on the bus tour or at Camp Casey III in Covington, Louisiana. If everyone who believes that our country can change from a paradigm of war to one of peace would do even did a small fraction of what our Camp Casey loyalists are doing, the war would be over tomorrow, the troops would be home, and America would be a safe and sane place to live. I honor everyone who works for peace, but especially the people who have dropped everything to take back our country and make it a better place to live and raise children.

In Columbia, South Carolina, yesterday, the Southern Leg of the Bus Tour spoke to a few hundred supporters and two counter protestors. One of the counter protestors had a sign that said "Support the Mission." I invited her to talk to me after the rally to explain what this ever-changing and ephemeral mission is now. She didn't. We all know that on August 29, George said that we need to stay in Iraq to keep the oil fields from falling into the hands of terrorists. Is that the mission? Are we supporting our troops dying and innocent Iraqi people being killed for oil and greed? This doesn't sound like anything I want to support.

Today in Raleigh there was a We Support the Troops rally while we were holding our We *Really* Support the Troops rally. I wonder if the people who say they support the troops by wanting to support more of them being killed realize how ironic that is. Is sending the troops—without proper body armor, proper vehicle armor, proper training, equipment, food, water, competent leadership, and support when they return home—to a mistaken war based on lies to occupy a country that was absolutely no threat to the United States really supporting them? These people equate supporting an evil mission with supporting the troops. I believe that the people on the peace side are the ones who authentically support the troops—by wanting them to come home alive! One sign said, "The Peace Symbol is the Footprint of the American Chicken." Don't they realize that they are protesting a group of people who have actually served our country in war, families who have loved ones serving, and families whose brave children have been killed for the deceptions of this criminal administration? And that the people who are sending our lifeblood off to kill and die *never* served their country in the military and don't have children in the military? They say, "Cindy doesn't speak for me." I wouldn't presume to speak for their narrow world view.

Another thing these pro-war people don't realize is that, just like them, we have the right to say what we are saying. We give them space to do so, and we would like the same space from them. Besides, if they think they are going to make us go away by protesting us, they are wrong. The number of pro-war, pro-Bush (sorry for being redundant) people is dwindling in numbers and intensity. Maybe the crimes that are happening in Louisiana have softened their venom? It is one thing for the criminal negligence of George and company to kill innocent Iraqis, but also killing innocent Americans in America, maybe that's where they draw the line. I hope the line is drawn quickly before George is allowed to harm more of us.

The "Winter Soldiers" who stayed in Crawford to guard the memorial to Casey, Camp Casey, and all of our fallen heroes, have reported two disturbing events. In the first, the McClennan County Board of Supervisors banned parking on county roads up to the Bush ranch. The supervisors had told us it was "private property," so I don't think they actually have any authority up Prairie Chapel Road. When we take Camp Casey back, I hope they don't try to stop us from parking there. If they do, maybe Fred will let us use his land to park, also.

The other thing that happened at Camp Casey: Some "patriot" stole the memorial. They took everything that honored our children. They stole Casey's boots. What will these people stop at? They are shameless, and they have no sense of moral values. In August, they tried to stop us by shooting rifles, mowing down the crosses, and calling us names. You know what? Nothing will stop us.

Even with the minor counter-protests, our spirits are high, and we are overwhelmed and grateful for all of the support we are getting from the true Americans who come out to help us bring the troops home now!

IT IS TIME TO START PUMPING HOPE INTO OUR OWN COMMUNITIES

Saturday, September 17

It has been one month, one week, and four days since I arrived in Crawford, Texas, and was sitting in a ditch there. My request was simple: I wanted to speak to the man who has sent over a million of our young people to fight, kill, and die in a country that was absolutely no threat to the United States of America. I wanted to ask him, "What is the Noble Cause that you keep talking about?"

We all know that George Bush never came down the road to talk to me. Thank God! People have been saying that I am the "spark," "catalyst," "face of the antiwar movement," etc. I beg to differ. George Bush and his arrogant advisers are the sparks that lit the prairie fire of peace activism that has swept over America and the entire world. If he had met with me that fateful day in August, it would not have been good for him (because I knew he was going to lie and I would have advertised that fact), but it would have had less of an impact on the peace movement if he had.

Reflecting on the events of August, I have come up with two reasons why George could not meet with me: (1) He is a coward, and (2) there is no Noble Cause. As I've said, if George had as much courage and integrity in his entire body as Casey had in his pinky, he would have met with me. But if he did have that much courage and integrity, he never would have preemptively invaded a practically defenseless country. His sycophantic cabinet and hangers-on are also incontrovertible evidence that he is a coward. No one had better dare disagree with him. How dare a mom from Vacaville, California, have the nerve to contradict the emperor of Prairie Chapel Road!

All of the "Noble Cause" reasons that George has given for the invasion and continued illegal occupation of a sovereign nation are patently false and ridiculous. He has been claiming recently (since he admitted a long time ago that Iraq had no WMDs or links to 9/11) that this occupation of Iraq is spreading "freedom and democracy" in the Middle East. Really? Does he have any idea that the constitution that the Iraqi governing body is working on is based on Sharia and that it undermines the freedoms of women? Does he realize that for over fifty years women have had equal rights with men in Iraq? Does George realize (of course he does) that the puppet government the U.S. put in place in Iraq is comprised of the very same people who encouraged the invasion to line their own pockets? What kind of freedom and democracy is this? If George is so hell-bent on freedom and democracy for Iraq, why doesn't he practice it here in America? Sixty-two percent of Americans believe that what George has done in Iraq is a mistake and we should begin to bring our troops home. Well, George, sixty-two percent is a clear majority and you should begin to listen to the people who pay your salary.

He has also claimed that what we are doing in Iraq is "making America safer." This statement is easier to disprove than the "freedom and democracy" baloney. To see through this deception, just look at the Gulf States. Ask the people of New Orleans if they feel safer. By misappropriating all of our personnel and equipment, and pouring billions of dollars into the sands of Iraq, George has made our country *more* vulnerable to attack by outside forces. If you listen to the cold and callous statements of people like Michael Chertoff and George's own mama, the people of New Orleans seem to be acceptable collateral damage to the country's ruling elite. It is my humble opinion that the only thing that will make America safer is to get

George and his unfeeling and dangerously incompetent supporters out of our White House.

We all now know the reason that we are in Iraq. George told us so from a break he was taking from Crawford in San Diego on the same day that Katrina was hitting the Gulf States. It is for oil. It is so that George, Dick, and their evil buddies can extract more profits from our children's flesh and blood. This is not a Noble Cause. As a matter of fact, it is the most ignoble cause for a war that has ever been waged. We as Americans knew, either in the front of our brains or in the back of our consciousness, that this war was to feed the corporations. Fifteen brave young Americans have been killed so far this month, while our attention has been focused, and rightfully so, on the Gulf States. Over two hundred innocent and unfortunate Iraqis have been killed this week alone. How much more blood are we as Americans going to allow George, Congress, and the corporations to spill before we demand an end to this war and an accounting for the lives that have been needlessly ruined?

It is time to stop hemorrhaging money in Iraq. I witnessed the abject poverty and sense of abandonment the less fortunate people of New Orleans were living in even before the levees broke. It is time to start pumping hope back into our own communities. It is time to start taking care of Americans. How many millions of our tax dollars are we going to allow George, Congress, and the corporations to misuse and waste in Iraq?

Not one more drop of blood. Not one more life. Not one more penny for killing.

If you love our country and want to see a change for the better, stand up and be counted for peace. The entire world is counting on you.

IRAQ AND KATRINA:
FAILED BOOKENDS OF A BUSH PRESIDENCY

Monday, September 19

"We have come to cash this check—a check that will give us upon demand the riches of freedom and the security of justice. We have also come to this hallowed spot to remind America of the fierce urgency of now. This is no time to engage in the luxury of cooling off or to take the tranquilizing drug of gradualism." —MARTIN LUTHER KING JR., "I HAVE A DREAM," AUGUST 28, 1963

Bush's Katrina shows once again that my son died for nothing. If you listen to Bush—and fewer and fewer are, thank goodness— we are in Iraq in part due to 9/11. All our president has been talking about has been protecting this country since 9/11. That's why people voted for him in the last election. Katrina shows it's all a sham, a fraud, a disaster as large as Katrina itself.

Hundreds of billions of dollars and tens of thousands of innocent lives later, what have we achieved? Nothing. Casey died for nothing, and Bush says others have to die for those that have died already.

Enough, George! What is disgusting is not, as the first lady says, criticism of you, but rather the crimes you've committed against this country and our sons and daughters. Stop hiding behind your twisted idea of God, and stop destroying this country.

This week I arrive in Washington D.C. to begin my vigil at the White House, just as I did in Texas. But this time I'll be joined by Katrina victims, as well. In your America we are all victims. The failed bookends of your Presidency are Iraq and Katrina.

It is time for all of us to stand up and be counted: to show the media, Congress, and this inept, corrupt, and criminal administration that we mean business. It is time to get off of our collective behinds to show the people who are running our country into oblivion that we will stand for it no longer; that we want our country back and we want our nation's young people back home, safe and sound, on our shores to help protect America; that it is time for a change in our country's "leadership"; that we will never go away until our dreams are reality.

There are so-called leaders in our country who are waiting for the correct, "politically expedient" time to speak up and out against the occupation of Iraq. It is no sweat for our politicos to wait for the right time, because not one of them has a child in harm's way. I don't care if the politician is a Democrat or a Republican, this is not about politics. Being a strong leader to guide our country out of the quagmire and mistake of Iraq will require people of courage and determination to stand up and say, "I don't care if I win the next election, people are dying in Iraq every day and families are being decimated." We, as the sixty-two percent of Americans who want our troops to begin coming home, will follow such a leader down the difficult but oh-so-rewarding path of peace with justice.

There is no longer time for the tranquilizing drug of gradualism. There never has been time for that. Our "now" is so fiercely urgent. Like my daughter, Carly, wrote in the last verse of her "A Nation Rocked to Sleep" poem:

> Have you ever heard the sound of a Nation Being
> Rocked to Sleep?
> Our leaders want to keep us numb so the pain won't
> be too deep,
> But if we the people allow them to continue, another
> mother will weep,
> Have you heard the sound of a Nation Being Rocked
> to Sleep?
> Wake up!

NOT ONE MORE MOTHER'S CHILD

Speech Given to 300,000 Protestors, Washington, D.C.

Saturday, September 24

We need a people's movement to end this war. My good friends in the media aren't doing their jobs. Most of our friends in Congress aren't doing their jobs. George Bush certainly isn't doing his job. So, you know what—we have to do our jobs, as Americans. If no one else will hold them accountable, we will. We'll do our job. We'll be the checks and balances on this out-of-control, criminal government, We are here in massive numbers to show our government, to show our media, to show America that we mean business. And we're not going home until every last one of our troops is home.

Everyone is coming up to me and saying, "Thank you for being here." Thank *you* for being here. If it weren't for the thousands and thousands of people who came to Camp Casey and the millions of people who supported us, I would still be sitting in that ditch. But you guys got me out of the ditch. You got us to our nation's capital, and we mean business, George Bush!

Now we're going to Congress, and we're going to ask, "How many more of other people's children are you willing to sacrifice for the lies?" And we're going to say, "Shame on you. Shame on you for giving him the authority to invade Iraq." And we're going to say, "Not one person should have died. Not one more should die." Can you scream that to the White House? Not one more! Not one more! Not one more!

Thank you. I love you.

WE DON'T EXIST

Saturday, September 24

Last weekend, Karl Rove said that I was a clown and that the antiwar movement was "nonexistent." I wonder if the hundreds of thousands of people who showed up today to protest this war and George's failed policies know that they don't exist. It is incredible that Karl thinks that he can wish us away by saying we aren't real. Well, Karl and Co., we are real, we do exist, and we are not going away until this illegal and immoral occupation of Iraq is over and you are sent back to the depths of whatever slimy, dark, and loathsome place you came from. I may be a clown, Karl, but you are about to be indicted. You preside over one of the biggest three-ring, malevolent circuses of all time: the Bush administration.

The rally today was overwhelming and powerful. The reports that I was arrested today were obviously false. The peace rally was mostly very peaceful. Washington, D.C., was filled with energetic and proud Americans who came from all over to raise their voices in unison against the criminals who run our government and their disastrous policies that are making our nation more vulnerable to all kinds of attacks (natural and Bush-made disasters). I was especially thrilled at the number of young people who came out—another sign that the side of good is winning.

I led the march for peace alongside such venerable activists as the Reverends Al Sharpton, Bob Edgars, and Jesse Jackson, and Julian Bond. Two of our congresswomen with *cajones*, Barbara Lee and Lynn Woolsey of California, also led the march. With the reverends, we stopped in front of the White House and said a prayer. After the prayer, I said that we are light and they are darkness. Darkness can *never* overcome the light, ever. As long as there is one spark, the darkness has lost. We will prevail. We will be victorious. The darkness has lost, because our beacons of peace and truth are shining for the entire world to see. And it is a very pretty sight.

Many people told me, "Thank you for coming." I want to tell America, "Thank you!!" At the Camp Casey reunion this evening, I was so overcome with emotion and gratitude that I wanted to hug every citizen of this country. We in the Camp Casey movement are so proud and thrilled that America showed up in such great numbers.

So much happened today! I am exhausted but very content. I am again filled with a renewed sense of hope that we will get our country back and get our troops home.

MY FIRST TIME

Monday, September 26

This time the rumors are true. I was arrested today in front of the White House, my first time ever being arrested.

We proceeded from Lafayette Park, across the street from the White House, to the Guard House by the White House gate. My sister Dede, Gold Star Families for Peace members, other Military Families, and I requested to meet with the president again. We still want to know: What is the Noble Cause? To our shock and surprise, our request was denied. They wouldn't even deliver letters or pictures of our killed, loved ones to the White House.

We all know that George hates it when people disagree with him. Even more, he is in denial that it even happens. Second, he is a coward who arrogantly refuses to meet with the people who pay his salary. And the third reason he won't talk to us is that he knows there is no Noble Cause for the invasion and continued occupation of Iraq. It's a question that has no true answer.

After we were refused a meeting with the Disconnected One, we sat down in front of our house, the White House, and refused to move until George came out and talked to us. We had a good time singing old church songs and old protest songs while we waited. I tied a picture of Casey on the White House fence, and apparently that is against the law, too.

After three warnings to get up and move off of the sidewalk, we were arrested. It is ironic to me that the person who resides in our White House swears to uphold and defend the Constitution of the United States of America has no concept of the Constitution. He was appointed by the Supreme Court for his first term, invaded and continues to occupy a sovereign country without a declaration of war from Congress, violated international treaties to invade Iraq, and condones the torture that pervades military prisons. These are all violations of the Constitution. The Patriot Act is a breach of the Bill of Rights. Denying us our right to peaceably assemble is a breach of the Bill of Rights. George is so hypocritically concerned about developing a Constitution for Iraq, while he ignores and shreds our own.

Being arrested wasn't a big deal. Even though we were arrested for "demonstrating without a permit," we were protesting something much more serious than sitting on a sidewalk. We were protesting the tragic and needless deaths of tens of thousands of innocent Iraqis and Americans, both in Iraq and here in America, who would be alive today if it weren't for the criminals who reside in and work in the White House.

Karl Rove outed a CIA agent and was responsible for endangering many of our covert agents worldwide. Dick Cheney's old company is reaping profits beyond anyone's wildest imaginations in their no-bid contracts in Iraq, Afghanistan, and New Orleans. John Negroponte was an ambassador in Central America during very shady and murderous times. Rumsfeld and Gonzales are responsible for the illegal and immoral authorization, encouragement, and approval of torture. Besides violating the Geneva Conventions, torture endangers the lives of our service men and women in Iraq. And Condi lied through her teeth in the insane run-up to the invasion. The list of crimes this administration has committed is extensive and abhorrent. It is so unbelievable that we were arrested for exercising our First Amendment rights, while these people are running free to enjoy their lives of crime and wreak havoc on the world.

The fine for "demonstrating without a permit" is $75. I certainly won't pay it. My court date is November 16.

VI.

THE CAMP CASEY MOVEMENT WILL NOT DIE

What is the noble cause that he says my son died for? The answer to that question will not bring my son back, but it may stop more meaningless deaths. The Camp Casey movement will not die until we have a genuine accounting of the truth and until our troops are brought home.

WHY I MUST TELL THE PRESIDENT AND THE CONGRESS TO STOP THE WAR

I will never, ever forget the night of April 4, 2004, when I found out that my son Casey had been killed in Iraq.

I will also never forget the day when we buried my sweet boy, my oldest son. If I live to be a very old lady and forget everything else, I will never forget when the general handed me the folded flag that had lain on Casey's coffin, as his brother and sisters, standing behind me, sobbed.

I think of Casey every day.

I waited outside President Bush's ranch in Crawford, Texas, for nearly a month, determined to meet with him.

I want to let the president know that I feel he recklessly endangered the life of my son by sending our troops to attack and occupy a country that was not an imminent threat to the United States.

And I want to let him know that millions of Americans believe that the best thing we can do—for our own security, for our soldiers, and for the Iraqi people—is to bring the U.S. troops home from Iraq now.

Just because it's too late for Casey and the Sheehan family, why would we want another innocent life taken in the name of this ever-changing and unwinnable mission in Iraq?

I did get to meet with President Bush two-and-a-half months after my son was killed, but I never got to say any of these things to him. I was in deep shock and grief at the time, and all I wanted to do was to show him pictures of Casey and tell him what a wonderful man our son was.

But today things are very different. My shock has worn off, and now I've got a lot of anger along with my grief.

I'm angry because every reason the Bush administration gave for the invasion of Iraq has been shown to be false.

The September 11 Commission Report concluded there was no link between Iraq and the September 11, 2001, attacks.

The weapons inspectors gave up searching for weapons of mass destruction and wrote in the Duelfer report that there were none to be found.

From the Downing Street Memo, we learned that the Bush administration "fixed'" intelligence to justify the Iraq invasion.

And after every supposed milestone in Iraq—the capture of Saddam Hussein, the transition to Iraqi rule, and most recently the Iraq election—things just don't get better. U.S. soldiers and Iraqis continue to be killed in greater and greater numbers, the cost of the war skyrockets, and there's no end in sight.

After thirty U.S. service members were killed in late July 2005, the president reiterated his pledge to complete the mission of our fallen soldiers. But that mission originally was to protect the United States from a lethal attack by Saddam Hussein—with weapons it turns out he did not have.

I don't want the president to use Casey's memory to justify continuing this war, which will end up only needlessly killing more wonderful young men like him.

Thousands of people streamed into Crawford to support my vigil and persuade the president to listen to the people who want an end to this war. We camped out in a drainage ditch, in 100-degree weather, but it was worth it.

If and when I do meet with the president, it will be for all of the Gold Star Families for Peace who lost children in this war, for all of the mothers and fathers and husbands and wives who are grieving and who want to tell the president to end this devastating war.

No one else—not one more mom—should have to lose her son in Iraq.

WHAT KIND OF EXTREMIST WILL YOU BE?

Early morning, April 4
Shot rings out in the Memphis sky
Free at last, they took your life
They could not take your pride
In the name of love!
What more in the name of love?

U2, "Pride (In the Name of Love)"

Most everyone reading this knows what happened to Dr. Martin Luther King, Jr. on April 4, 1968. And most of you now know what happened to my son Spc. Casey Austin Sheehan on April 4, 2004. Dr. King and Casey were murdered by the same malevolent ideologies that say that we have to be mortally afraid of the "ism" du jour and we, as Americans who have the "moral high ground" in the world, can send our innocent children to invade innocent countries and kill innocent people to fight the "ists" that go with the "isms." In Vietnam we were fighting the evil Communists, and in Iraq we are fighting the evil Terrorists. By the late 1980s our war against Communism had outstayed its welcome and the military-industrial war complex had run out of excuses to build bombs, tanks, bullets, ships, submarines, and soldiers. So, in 2001, our leaders who serve the war machine had to switch our enemy to Terrorism.

Dr. King had the temerity to challenge the war machine and war racketeers in his famous speech at Riverside Church in New York on April 4, 1967, and he paid for that bit of inspired, courageous honesty with his life, exactly one year later. Casey had the naïve gall to join the U.S. Army thinking he would be making the world a better, safer place, and he paid for that immature but honest patriotic mistake with his wonderful life.

Casey was a brave and honorable man who, we were told, volunteered to go on the mission that killed him to save the lives of his buddies. He was shot in the back of the head and died a little while later in a medic's station while a medic was trying to hold his brains in while the doctors tried to keep him breathing. We have heard wildly disparate stories of Casey's last few minutes on earth. I don't know if we will ever know the truth. One thing I do know is that like Dr. King, Casey's murder will be to advance the cause for peace in the name of love.

I am wholly and completely convinced that this aggression on Iraq is illegal, immoral, and appallingly unnecessary. I am also convinced that one drop of blood is one drop of blood too much to be shed for this abomination in Iraq. Now oceans of blood—both Iraqi and American—have been spilled for ruinous and disturbing policies of very bad people in our government who have based their reasons for invasion and occupation on their twisted imaginations and their seemingly bottomless lust for power, profits, chaos, and confusion.

Martin Luther King, Jr. wrote this from the Birmingham Jail in 1963, and it is so relevant today: "We will have to repent in this generation not merely for the hateful words and actions of bad people, but for the appalling silence of the good people."

I regretfully admit that before my son was killed, I didn't speak out publicly against the invasion and occupation of Iraq.

I didn't shout out and say, "Stop! Stop this insane rush to an invasion that has no basis in reality. Don't invade a country based on cherry-picked, prefabricated intelligence and contemptible scare tactics!"

I didn't stand up and scream, "Congress, don't you dare abrogate your constitutional rights and responsibilities! Do not, under *any* circumstances give the keys to our country to power-drunk, irresponsible, and reckless maniacs!"

When George threateningly stated in his disordered and defiant headlong rush to disaster, "If you're not for us, you're against us," I will regret forever not calling him on the phone and screaming, "I am *so* against you and your repulsive policies, you self-important man. I am against killing innocent people, and I am against you telling me it's unpatriotic to be against you and your murderous philosophy!"

Why, oh why, was I silent when the cowardly and capricious armchair warriors of the Pentagon sent my son and over a million other brave young Americans to an atrocious excuse (that never should have been fought in the first place) for a war without the proper equipment, armor, training, supplies, or planning? I should have boldly strode up the Pentagon and said, "Look here, Donald, not only do you not go to war with the Army you 'have,' you make sure our precious lifeblood is well protected if you do send them off to fight. And how about not sending our kids to die in the sand or soil of another country *unless* it is absolutely necessary to defend our own sand and soil?"

If I had broken the bonds of my slavery to silence sooner, would Casey (and scores of others) still be alive? I don't know. There were and still are so many good people working for peace and justice, and they have been for many years. I do know that no matter how much I scream and cry and rail against God, country, and humanity, I cannot bring Casey back. But I have not shut up since Casey was killed, nor will I be silent until every last one of our nation's sons and daughters is brought back from this morally repugnant and ill-fated war! Nor will I give up when this occupation is finished. I will continue fighting for the children of the world to make sure that a tragedy of historic proportions like this never happens again. If I can save even one mother here or there from the pain and agony I'm going through, it will have been so immensely worth it.

I encourage and challenge every citizen of the world to do one small thing for peace each day. You can nag your elected officials to demand the keys of our country back from the all-but-convicted felons, liars, and self-proclaimed pro-life hypocrites who have them now.

Casey and Dr. King were violently killed on April 4 in different years, during different wars, but these two wars are just different sides of the same coin. I want their deaths to mean something, to count for peace and justice, and not violence and hatred.

Every day, I feel my son's presence urging me on to save his buddies. I hear him whispering in my ear and in my dreams, "Mom, finish my mission. Bring my buddies home alive." And I can hear Dr. King's words similarly challenging me to action: "The question is not whether we will be extremists, but what kind of extremists will we be."

Casey, my son, my hero, Dr. King, the hero of millions, I pledge to be the kind of extremist who works for peace with justice and who will never take "no" for an answer. I will strive to hold the people in our government accountable for all of the heartache and emptiness they have caused our world by their deliberate lies and deceptions and by their misuse of power and abuse of our nation's precious human resources. I will be the kind of extremist who believes that our country can be taken back from the corporatocracy and unethical war profiteers that control it now. I will be the kind of extremist who believes that the people of Iraq can rebuild their own country without the dangerous "help" of the American military, and I will be the kind of extremist who works unceasingly to bring our kids home from the Middle East immediately!

If there was ever a time in our nation's history that the passion and compassion of extremists are needed, it is now. This very minute.

What kind of extremist will you be?

FROM DESPAIR TO HOPE

For many nights after Casey was killed and we buried him, I had to restrain myself from swallowing my entire bottle of sleeping pills. The pain and the deep pit of hopelessness and despair were almost more than I could cope with. How can a person be expected to live in a world that is so full of pain and devoid of hope? I would think to myself, "It would be so easy to take these pills and go to sleep and never wake up in this awful world again."

The only thing that restrained me from committing the cowardly and selfish act of killing myself was my other three children. How could I put them through something so horrible after what they had already been through? I knew I had to live and that living was going to be (and still is) the hardest thing I'll ever have to do.

I know now why some people do kill themselves—it is the lack of hope. For me it was the black pit of knowing that I would have to wake up every day for the rest of my life with the pain of knowing I will never see Casey again, that I will have to exist in a world without him—and just existing is no way to live.

Then, three weeks after Casey was killed, my daughter Carly came out and hit me with my reason for living. She read to me a poem she had written, "A Nation Rocked to Sleep":

Have you ever heard the sounds of a mother screaming
  for her son?
The torrential weeping of a mother will never be done,
They call him a hero, you should be glad he's one, but,
Have you ever heard the sound of a mother weeping
  for her son?

The first stanza reminded me that I was not the only one in the universe in such excruciating grief. But the verse that helped me claw my way out of the pit of despair, one agonizing inch at a time, was the last stanza:

Have you ever heard the sound of a nation being
  rocked to sleep?
The leaders want to keep you numb so the pain won't
  be so deep.
But if we the people let them continue, another mother
  will weep.
Have you ever heard the sounds of a nation being
  rocked to sleep?

When she recited those lines to me, I knew I would have to spend any amount time, money, and energy to try to bring the troops home before another mother would have to weep. I felt ashamed that I hadn't tried to stop the war before Casey died. Foolishly, I'd thought, "What can one person do?" Now I knew that even if I couldn't make a difference, I could at least try. If I failed, I would be able to go to my grave knowing that I had given it my very best shot. So, I vowed to try.

Gradually, I started to get three doses of hope back, and then slide two doses back. I had a marvelous time in Florida campaigning against George Bush. I founded Gold Star Families for Peace. I was a main speaker at the Peace Rally in Fayetteville, North Carolina. Casey and I were on the cover of *The Nation* magazine. I testified at Congressman John Conyers' Downing Street Memo hearings in June 2005. I could feel that, one chip at a time, I was helping erode public support for the occupation of Iraq.

Then, in August of 2005, after I had already separated from my husband of twenty-eight years, I was at home watching TV (a very rare occurrence), and I saw that fourteen Marines from Ohio were killed in a single incident. If that weren't heartbreaking and sickening enough, George Bush came on the TV and said that the families of fallen soldiers could rest assured that their loved ones had died for "a noble cause." That enraged me and inflamed my sense of failure. Even before Casey was killed, certainly after he was killed, and on that day—August 3, 2005—I did not believe that invading a country that was about as much threat to the USA as Switzerland, killing tens of thousands of innocent people all for greed for power and money, is a noble cause. I decided to go to Crawford to ask him what the "noble cause" is.

Then George had the unfortunate temerity to say, "Complete the mission to honor the sacrifices of the fallen." For months, I had been calling for him to stop saying that, and it enraged me to hear it again. I don't want one more mother to have her heart and soul ripped out of her for no reason, for lies and crap. I wanted to go to Crawford to demand that George quit using my son's honorable and courageous sacrifice to continue his dishonorable and cowardly killing.

The rest is history. The more the American people learned about and came to Camp Casey and the more letters, cards, emails, phone calls, and packages of support we received, the happier we at Camp Casey became. We realized something that we had forgotten after almost five years of living in the virtual dictatorship of control we have in America now. We realized that "We the People" have all the power! We only *need* to exercise our rights and responsibilities as Americans to dissent from an irresponsible, reckless, ignorant, and arrogant government. We realized, a little late but not too late, that when George said, "If you're not for us, you're against us," we all should have risen in angry, righteous, and patriotic unison and said, "You are damn right you lying, out-of-control madman. We are so against you and your insane rush to invade Iraq!"

We didn't rise up then, but Camp Casey taught us that it is not just okay, it is *mandatory* to raise our voices against the government when the government is responsible for killing innocents. It is mandatory that when the checks and balances supposedly in place are not functioning for "We the People" to *be* the checks and balances on the media and the government.

I had thought all my hope was KIA the day Casey was KIA. Carly's poem gave me a *reason* to live. Camp Casey, with its wonderful feelings of love, acceptance, peace, community, joy, and, yes, optimism for our future, gave me back my *desire* to live. I can smile and laugh now and even mean it most of the time—things we often take for granted, but I never will again.

Living with hope that our world will one day exist in a paradigm of peace, love, and nonviolent conflict resolution is a very good way to exist. I love being alive now and will devote my life to peace with justice so our children will never, ever be misused by the war machine again.

Thank you, America.

Thank you, Casey.

Resources
for Action
and Education

RESOURCES FOR ACTION
AND EDUCATION

Here is a list of some of the organizations and independent media working for peace and keeping the public informed.

Groups Working for Peace

BRING THEM HOME NOW TOUR: military families who have lost loved ones in Iraq and Afghanistan or have loved ones in harm's way and veterans of the wars in Iraq and Vietnam have joined together to tell their stories and to call on this administration and congress to end the war and bring our troops home now. www.bringthemhomenowtour.org

CODEPINK: WOMEN FOR PEACE: a grassroots peace and social justice movement seeking positive social change through proactive, creative protest and nonviolent direct action, calling on women and men around the world to rise up and oppose the war in Iraq. www.codepink4peace.org

MEET WITH CINDY: formed to persuade President Bush to meet with Cindy Sheehan and answer her questions about why the war that took Casey's life was started and why it is being continued. www.meetwithcindy.org

MEET WITH THE MOTHERS: formed by individuals to spread the spirit, power, and love of Camp Casey and to bring Cindy Sheehan's call for answers about the war to Congressmembers, who have the power to stop the war. Sponsored by Gold Star Families for Peace. www.meetwiththemothers.org

NOT ONE MORE: individuals taking Cindy Sheehan's questions to governors, members of congress, and others who have the power to stop the war. Not One More Lie, Not One More Day, Not One More Dollar, Not One More Life. Sponsored by Gold Star Families for Peace. www.notonemore.com

TRUE MAJORITY: a grassroots education and advocacy project that takes action on issues based on compassion, charity, and justice, the values we must adhere to in order to build a safer, more secure home and world. www.truemajority.org

UNITED FOR PEACE AND JUSTICE: 1300 groups joined together to oppose the U.S. government's policy of permanent warfare and empire building. www.unitedforpeace.org

Members of the Military and their Families Working for Peace

ARLINGTON WEST: On a Sunday morning in late 2003, a group of Veterans for Peace in Santa Barbara erected small white crosses on the beach, one for every soldier killed in Iraq. The next Sunday, they did it again. And the Sunday after that. As the number of crosses grew, photos, flowers, and flags were added. What began as a political statement became a shrine. Since then, Arlington Wests have been erected in other cities, and at Camp Casey in Texas.
www.veteransforpeace.org/Arlington_west_121003.htm

CASEY'S PEACE PAGE:
www.angelfire.com/sk3/spkhntrca/Casey.html

GOLD STAR FAMILIES FOR PEACE: families who have suffered the tragic loss of a child in war organized to raise awareness about the true human costs of the invasion of Iraq, to bring an end to the occupation, and to reach out to other families who have lost loved ones as a result of war. gsfp.org

IRAQ VETERANS AGAINST THE WAR: veterans who served since 9/11/01 who are committed to the immediate withdrawal of all occupying forces in Iraq and to making sure all veterans receive the benefits owed them. www.ivaw.net

MILITARY FAMILIES SPEAK OUT: relatives and loved ones of those in the military who are opposed to the war in Iraq. www.mfso.org

VETERANS FOR PEACE: veterans—drawing on their unique experiences and perspectives—committed to raising public awareness of the true costs and consequences of militarism and war and to seeking peaceful, effective alternatives. www.veteransforpeace.org

News and Information Sources

For democracy to work, we need access to independent, diverse sources of news and information. Following are a few of the many alternatives to the mainstream media.

BROADCAST

AIR AMERICA RADIO: a liberal radio network featuring presentations, interviews, listeners' calls, and news. Featuring Al Franken, Randi Rhodes, Thom Hartmann, Laura Flanders, and others. www.airamericaradio.com

DEMOCRACY NOW! a daily news program, hosted by Amy Goodman and Juan Gonzales, offering access to rarely heard people and perspectives. Airs on over 375 radio and TV stations. www.democracynow.org

FREE SPEECH TV: independent national TV channel that reflects diversity, provides underrepresented perspectives, and encourages citizens to work for change. On DISH Satellite Network. www.freespeech.org

INDEPENDENT MEDIA CENTER: a collective of independent media organizations and journalists offering grassroots, non-corporate coverage for the creation of radical, accurate, and passionate tellings of the truth. www.indymedia.org

LINK TV: offers in-depth programs with a global perspective, giving voice to the voiceless and encouraging action on the part of the viewer. On DIRECTV, DISH Satellite Network, and Direct Broadcast Satellite Television. www.worldlinktv.org

NEWS SOURCES ON THE WEB

AFTER DOWNING STREET: www.afterdowningstreet.org

ALTER NET: www.alternet.org

BUZZ FLASH: www.buzzflash.com

COMMON DREAMS: www.commondreams.org

DAHR JAMAIL'S IRAQ DISPATCHES: www.dahrjamailiraq.com

HUFFINGTON POST: www.huffingtonpost.com

MICHAEL MOORE: www.michaelmoore.com

TOM DISPATCH: www.tomdispatch.org

TRUTHOUT: www.truthout.org

ZNET: www.znet.org

NATIONAL MAGAZINES

The Nation: www.thenation.com

The Progressive: www.progressive.org

Mother Jones: www.motherjones.com

Utne: www.utne.com

Photo Credits

COURTESY OF DEDE MILLER: Sheehan Family Photos (p. 86).

JEFF PATERSON/NOT IN OUR NAME: Cindy Sheehan, Martin Sheen, and Iraq Veterans Against the War (cover), Ken Ballard's Cross (p. 87); Joan Baez, Rancher, Gold Star Families for Peace (p. 88); Three Women, Cindy with Rev. Al Sharpton (p. 89); Cindy with Ruben Flores, Morning Press Conference (p. 90); Cindy with Tomas Young and IVAW, Veteran with Candle (p. 91). See www.notinourname.net/war/sheehan.htm.

ALASKA GYRL: Tent at Camp Casey II (pp. 88-89). See http://alaskagyrl.blogspot.com.

AP PHOTOS/LM OTERO: Cindy in Front of Caravan (p. 85); Cindy at Casey's Cross (p. 87); Cindy Aboard Bus (p. 91).

AP PHOTO/TONY GUTIERREZ: Volunteers Placing Crosses (p. 87).

AP PHOTO/DONNA MCWILLIAM: Banner Honoring Casey Sheehan (p. 90).

AP PHOTO/PABLO MARTINEZ MONSIVAIS: Cindy Arrested (p. 92).

REUTERS (CORBIS)/JASON REED: Cindy's D.C. Speech (p. 92).

About the Contributors

The Honorable John Conyers, Jr. has represented Michigan's 14th Congressional District since 1964. He is the second longest serving member of the U.S. House of Representatives, the ranking member of the House Judiciary Committee, cofounder of the Congressional Black Caucus, and a leading figure in the Democratic Party. In 2004, he convened hearings on alleged electoral improprieties in Ohio and in 2005 on the Downing Street Memo. He is the recipient of many awards including a Southern Christian Leadership Conference Award presented to him by Dr. Martin Luther King, Jr.

Thom Hartmann is an internationally best-selling, Project Censored Award–winning author, a lecturer on culture and communications, a talk show host on Air America and the Sirius Satellite Network, and an innovator in the fields of psychiatry, ecology, and democracy. Among his fourteen books in print are *The Last Hours of Ancient Sunlight*, *Thom Hartmann's Complete Guide to ADHD*, *What Would Jefferson Do?* and *Unequal Protection: The Rise of Corporate Dominance and the Theft of Human Rights*.

Jodie Evans has been a community, social, and political activist for more than thirty years. Among her many accomplishments, she served as California Governor Jerry Brown's Director of Administration, founded the Grief Recovery Center, ran Governor Brown's 1991 campaign for president based on political reform and $100 contribution limit, coproduced the World Festival of Sacred Music, and as cofounder of CODEPINK: Women for Peace, spent the month of August 2005 with Cindy Sheehan at Camp Casey. Jodie co-edited *Twilight of Empire* and *Stop the Next War Now* and is working on a book on spirit in action.

About the Author

Cindy Sheehan lost her son Army Specialist Casey Austin Sheehan, in an ambush in Sadr City, Baghdad, on April 4, 2004. In the months following, as information became available revealing how the war in Iraq was based on lies, Cindy began speaking out, demanding an end to the war and that the troops be brought home.

On August 6, 2005, Cindy Sheehan went to president Bush's ranch in Crawford, Texas, to ask the president what "noble cause" he's referring to when he speaks about the war, and she vowed to stay outside his ranch until met with her. Ten thousand people joined her vigil and formed a community known as Camp Casey. The presdient did not meet with Cindy, but because of her clarity, courage, and conviction, her efforts rejuvenated the antiwar movement in America. Cindy Sheehan is founder of Gold Star Families for Peace. She continues to devote her time and energy to ending the war.

About the Publisher

Koa Books publishes books on personal transformation, progressive politics, and native cultures. To sign up for our mailing list and be notified of future publications and special offers, please go to www.koabooks.com or send your postal and e-mail addresses to:

Koa Books
P.O. Box 6718
Santa Fe, NM 87502

www.koabooks.com